Season of Suffering

Season of Suffering

Coming of Age in Occupied France, 1940–45

Nicole H. Taflinger

Washington State University Press
Pullman, Washington

Washington State University Press
PO Box 645910
Pullman, Washington 99164-5910
Phone: 800-354-7360
Fax: 509-335-8568
E-mail: wsupress@wsu.edu
Web site: wsupress.wsu.edu

Library of Congress Cataloging-in-Publication Data

Taflinger, Nicole H., 1927-
   Season of suffering : coming of age in occupied France, 1940-45 / Nicole H. Taflinger.
      p. cm.
   ISBN 978-0-87422-305-7 (alk. paper)
   1. Taflinger, Nicole H., 1927--Childhood and youth. 2. Taflinger, Nicole H.,
1927--Family. 3. Teenage girls--France--Nancy--Biography. 4. Nancy (France)--
Biography. 5. Nancy (France)--Social life and customs--20th century. 6. Nancy (France)-
-History, Military--20th century. 7. World War, 1939-1945--Personal narratives, French.
8. World War, 1939-1945--Social aspects--France--Nancy. 9. France--History--German
occupation, 1940-1945. I. Title.
   DC801.N16T34 2010
   944'.38230816092--dc22
   [B]

                                                                           2010004255

Fine Quality Books from the Pacific Northwest

Dedicated to

Ancel Gordon Taflinger

Nicole Braux, late 1944.

T HE SPRING OF 1929 is just beginning and I'm not yet 2 years old. I'm in the front yard sitting on a low stone wall, holding onto the grill fencing. Once in awhile, I poke my fingers in the stitch design of my pinkish sweater.

This is my first recollection.

The house was my second residence, on Rue de la République in Laxou, a west-side suburb of Nancy in northeastern France. I was born Nicole Braux and our family originally lived in Savigny in the Vosges further eastward, of which I have no recollection (and didn't revisit until 1977).

Bittersweet

I remember the smell of egg whites frying in my special, tiny, black-iron skillet. I'd sit on the window sill eating them at noon after Grandmother Marie Braux patiently removed the yolks to make cakes for our restaurant on Rue Jeanne d'Arc in Nancy, where we next moved, closer to downtown. The window sill was a step above a glass awning over the sidewalk, covering the outer terrace of the café-restaurant. One day, I caused fear and excitement when stepping out on it, but all was well when I decided to back off to the window sill. The crowd that gathered clapped!

I must've been a trial to my parents and grandmother. I still hear the screeching sound of my father's saw as he removed a bar from our wrought iron banister. I'd squeezed my head between two of the bars and couldn't get out on my own.

The café-restaurant was quite a playground for me. I was small enough to walk under tables, but couldn't reach the glasses on top. Nevertheless, I'm told I earned quite a reputation for emptying peoples' beers or drinks when they left for the restrooms. I recall the smells of the zinc countertop and the huge coffee machine. Vienna waltzes on the "pick up" (phonograph) remain in my ears.

I watched tramways passing by, clinking along, but one day my heart broke when seeing my adored black and white kitten getting run over by one of them. My first encounter with death. My parents, who could do everything, fix anything, couldn't make it move again.

First Love, Guilt, Jealousy

Monsieur Huguin was tall and gentle, with red hair and beard, and spoke in a beautiful gentlemanly voice. As soon as he walked into the café-restaurant, I'd go sit at his table. He'd tell stories and order me a grenadine, since he probably didn't think I'd take a sip of his beer or wine. He was the first man to make me feel like a lady. I later learned he was an actor—his most important role, Jesus in the annual Passion play.

One day, Monsieur Huguin brought in a dog. Terrified by it, I hid behind the counter. Afterward, I wouldn't speak to him, which eventually caused me to feel guilt on top of sorrow. Later, when Monsieur Huguin didn't come for several days, my parents told me he'd died during a performance—we wouldn't see him again.

Jealousy struck me when another of our customers, Monsieur Jules, brought his wife for dinner. Worse yet, another day he came in with a baby carriage containing a tiny little girl. Even though Monsieur Jules wasn't handsome like Monsieur Huguin—he was a short, roly-poly man with thin, blond hair—I considered him a fair substitute for my affections until that fateful day.

Sixteen years later, I unexpectedly met him again. Just a few days before leaving France for a new life in America, I was waiting for the tram with my mother. When looking around, I saw this familiar looking man. I told mother and she herself had trouble remembering. We went up to him, introduced ourselves, and lo, it was Monsieur Jules. It was a delightful meeting. He remembered my pouting jealousy over his wife and baby.

I didn't have a crush on another man, Monsieur Wilt—his voice was too loud and he teased me. Also, I didn't appreciate it when he and father argued a lot. I learned later that Monsieur Wilt, being an artist and poor, couldn't pay for his room and board, the reason for their disputes.

Aside from Jeanette, our waitress, who was fired for taking money out of the till, I have no recollection of the other roomers and customers, only the feeling of always being surrounded by people and noise.

Grandmother Braux often took me to play in the nearby park, *Ste. Marie,* on the *esplanade* in front of the Beaux Arts school. It was a beautiful playground for me.

Braux Family

Marie Augustine Braux *(Grand'Mère Braux)* – Auguste Braux *(deceased)*

|

Marcel Braux *(only child, b. 1902) m.* Cécile Faucheur *(b. 1909)*

|

Nicole Braux *(only child, b. 5/11/1927)*

Hard Times and Illness

The Depression years proved difficult for my parents. Father wasn't a particularly good businessman—he allowed people too much credit. Having sold his farm and sawmill in Savigny to purchase our café-restaurant/hotel in Nancy, he soon found himself forced to sell it at a great loss. He then needed to look for employment in a city still somewhat foreign to him.

Nancy was my mother's birthplace. Savigny, where we resided before, was a small village in the mountains and life there had become difficult for her. She wasn't accepted by the long-established families and they eyed her with suspicion, especially when father brought electricity to this conservative, old-fashioned community that disapproved of change.

Father enjoyed city life and didn't regret his move, even though the business failure proved difficult for him and mother. Even in better economic times, he might not have been successful because of a lack of business acumen. For example, he didn't like the brand of beer he sold; therefore, he'd take friends across the street to drink at a competitor's café. This didn't encourage his customers to enjoy our beer. After nine months, we sold out and moved to an apartment on Rue du Général Duroc, not far from Rue Jeanne d'Arc.

The new owners of the café moved in the day we left. They had two lovely, blond girls, around 6 and 8 years old. We met for a very short time (I don't recall exactly how long, an hour possibly), but they made an extraordinary impression on me—a lasting one—as I still recall them vividly.

It was a gray, almost rainy day, about 10 o'clock in the morning, when I walked out of the café with Grandmother Braux, who lived with us. My parents had left earlier with the movers to our new apartment on #16 Rue du Général Duroc, about six or eight blocks away. I carried a small can of cream in my favorite container, my other hand holding grandmother's. As we walked across the street and started on our way, I heard the two little girls calling out to me from the sidewalk in front of the café: *T'es peut! T'es peut!* (French slang meaning "You are ugly! You are ugly!")

I believe this was the first time I became aware of my appearance. Grandmother did her best to console me as I cried all the way to our new home. I'd found the two girls so beautiful in their blondness. Being dark, short, and plump, nobody could convince me I'd ever look pretty. Terribly hurt, I wanted to hide in grandmother's skirt. I suppose the excitement of moving into our new home must've dispelled this sad experience.

"We resided on the fourth floor, #16 Rue du Général Duroc."

Rue du Général Duroc was a short street with houses built in the 19th century. Still visible were holes and indentations caused by bullets and shrapnel during World War I and the 1870–71 Prussian war. Our new life was quite different. Formerly, I had lots of freedom to roam around upstairs in our living area, in the café, and the big kitchen in back, as well as the in attic and cave (basement). At Rue du Général Duroc we had a much smaller living area. We resided on the 4th floor with tenants living below us, which of course meant making no noise! I wasn't to run, shout, or drop things. I was to become a quiet little girl.

We lived there until I was 10 (when we moved to Boulevard Foch). I enjoyed the bedroom's balconies overlooking Rue du Général Duroc, where I could see the tops of maple trees two stories below. Birds of all kinds nested and sang in the branches.

Another big thrill was watching soldiers marching along our street from barracks located a few blocks away. Mainly infantry and cavalry, they practiced maneuvers in nearby fields in the suburbs. They included soldiers from different ethnic groups of the French colonies. The "Annamites," today's Vietnamese, were so attractive to me with their slanted eyes. How I wanted eyes like them!

The most magnificent soldiers were the "Spahis," North Africans on small horses, wearing turbans and long capes. Black soldiers from Madagascar or the Cameroons always seemed affected by the cold—even in summer heat they donned winter coats. Women in the area knitted heavy sweaters and scarves for them. They shivered even in July.

Sometimes, I'd watch the soldiers from the sidewalk, but their horses looked enormous and frightened me. I always feared horses. Mother tried to make me like them because she'd rode bareback as a girl. Her favorite horse was deaf. She was the only one who rode him and she loved him very much. When it was sleeting one morning, some of the soldiers' horses slid and fell. I felt so sad about this, and angry at the men, who (it appeared to me) acted roughly when getting them up.

I was full of fantasies about soldiers and spies. On one occasion, I believed I spotted a "spy" when a man in a strange uniform—red stripe on the side of his trousers, long sword at his side, big feather in his hat, and wearing white gloves—entered a house across the street. When mother came home at noon, I told her to inform the police—there was a spy on our street. Deadly serious and worried, as a good citizen I felt we needed to do something about it. Mother pretended to go somewhere, and after coming back, she said she'd discovered he wasn't a spy, but a neighbor's son in his St. Cyr military academy uniform. I was disappointed. He would've been the most beautiful spy I'd ever seen.

My recollections of the early years in this apartment are mainly of fantasies. The balconies were my kingdoms. I thought I stood on top of a castle. I flew over the trees like the birds. In winter, I'd put an ear against a window pane, place a hand over my other ear, close my eyes, and pretend I was at sea in a storm. With the wind against the window being amplified, I'd hum mournful tunes in accompaniment.

I remained glued to the windows for several months, watching the steeple of the Notre Dame de Lourdes church being built two blocks away. It was incredible to watch men up so high on scaffolds. After they installed the clock, I learned to tell time from it. I still remember the great day when the weather cock was put on top and the bells rang for the first time. I believe I was about 5 years old.

"I learned to tell time from the clock on the Notre Dame de Lourdes steeple."

About this time, a flu and measles epidemic struck Europe. Many of the soldiers at the barracks took sick and died. I came down with the measles, too. Mother, who hadn't ever had measles, caught it from me. We became extremely ill. She almost died due to a high fever, and developed pleurisy. Meanwhile, I contracted bronchitis. As mother revived somewhat, I came down with pneumonia. With antibiotics unavailable in those times, my fate swung in the balance for nine days. I wasn't aware of this, but my parents later said they feared losing me. I recall one time, when having such a severe headache, I begged my parents to remove cauliflowers from under my pillow; they were hurting my head.

Finding a doctor proved difficult, as they were all so overworked. We put our trust in a young man who'd been practicing only a week. He became our most trusted and beloved family doctor. (Years later before I left for America, he was the one to inform me of my first pregnancy. Our farewell was most difficult for both of us.) Father told me many times how I owed my life to Dr. Polu.

His first call at our apartment came at 4 o'clock in the morning. He told my parents he barely had hope for me, but if they allowed him, he'd try a new remedy—an injection of turpentine in my thigh to draw the infection to that area. He stayed till mid-morning, bathing me in cold towels to lower my fever. Then he fell asleep on my parents' bed with me in his arms. (I've been told this, as I don't recall. I remained in a coma.)

Apparently the unusual treatment worked. My thigh swelled, the fever went down, I could breathe again, and I woke up screaming. The infected area needed lancing, but I wouldn't let Dr. Polu do it unless he promised to marry me. The minute I laid eyes on him, I fell in love with him. He promised to marry me, but I'd have to let him do what he needed to do. Then, when I was older, he'd marry me. For many years I kept asking Dr. Polu if I was old enough. I remained ill for months. He wrapped me in mustard packs, covering my entire body. It was atrocious. I don't think I could've watched it being done to my own children. But I lived.

Mother had a relapse, and contracted tuberculosis. This was a most difficult time for us. Money was short during the height of the Depression. Father worked overtime to pay our medical bills and grandmother became exhausted from taking care of us. We didn't go to the hospital; Dr. Polu felt we wouldn't receive good care due to the overcrowding. Mother was treated for her TB and survived.

In this period, four people came into my life who exerted

"Mother"—Cécile Faucheur Braux, June 1945.

the greatest influence in so many ways—Dr. Polu (a most beautiful man, who became head of Nancy's pulmonary hospital), two nuns whose duty at different times was to come every other day to give shots to mother and I, and Grandmother Marie Faucheur, who attended to us almost daily.

Sister Joseph was the first nun giving us shots. Always arriving short of breath after climbing the four flights of stairs, she needed a glass of wine or she simply couldn't give us our shots properly. Being a nun, she couldn't swear, but felt it alright to say *nom de diou* instead of *nom de dieu*, which was blasphemy. This shocked Grandmother Braux, who was extremely lady-like, proper, and religious; she didn't miss a day of mass. But it was greatly endearing to my other grandmother, who tried hard to say *nom de diou* when Sister Joseph visited. Both Sister Joseph and my Grandmother Faucheur became great friends, especially over their glass of wine.

Sister Joseph became concerned over how my illness prevented me from entering school. Children started school at the age of 5; I was nearly 6. She took it upon herself to teach me to read and count. I saw her every other day for about a year. After several relapses of bronchitis and asthma, but finally recovering, I could read, write, and do arithmetic at about the second grade level. Of course, most of my reading was religious in content—mainly the lives of saints, history (dealing with even more saints), Joan of Arc, St. Louis, and on and on. I also read fairy tales, of course, and magazines for children such as *Lisette, Fillette, Le Semaine de Suzette*, and dear *Bécassine*.

To Sister Joseph I owe my educational life—my love of reading—plus patience and numerous feelings without name, which have to do with a God who is for everybody and everything. You can even tell Him when you are mad at Him, which she did all the time! She gave and gave of herself for nothing in return, or for the largest thing one can get in return—to love God and people, and be loved in return.

One day when the bell rang, I dashed to the door expecting Sister Joseph and her curses about the stairs, but to my dismay the person standing before me wasn't the plump, short sister. All was silent. Was I ill again and delirious? Dreaming? In front of me stood a tall, slender, beautiful lady—in a nun's habit, surely, but not Sister Joseph. A princess, a saint, an angel. I didn't throw myself at her and hug her as with Sister Joseph. I just stood there and called for mother.

This beautiful woman was Sister Léon, replacing Sister Joseph who was ill. She'd come to administer our shots. If one can think of black and white, this was it. The shock became even greater when hearing her speak. I'd never heard such ladylike language. Such gentleness wasn't possible.

Sister Léon came regularly. Even though I greatly missed Sister Joseph, I never had enough of Sister Léon's visits. She was the princess in my fairy tales, the saint in my books. I loved her. She took over my education where Sister Joseph had left off, but with differences. My writing became legible, my hair brushed hundreds of times, my nails cut just right, and so on.

Mother and Grandmother didn't share my admiration—they respected Sister Léon because she demanded it. But now, what house cleaning sessions before her arrival! And no glass of wine for this lady! Grandmother Faucheur stopped coming on those days.

Mother and I went to visit Sister Joseph at the convent. She was dying. She was so glad to see us. She told us not to feel sad because she was so happy to see Jesus. We cried anyway—she'd been so much a part of our lives.

Sister Léon came less and less as mother and I no longer required shots. Aside from giving me lessons in grooming and reading, however, she saved me from deformity. After lying ill in bed for so long, my back became deformed, with one of the shoulder blades out of place. Dr. Polu suggested surgery in the future, which we couldn't afford. National health insurance hadn't yet been instituted in France and we were extremely poor. Sister Léon had an idea. Though it caused me months of pain and misery, we had nothing to lose. Dr. Polu agreed to give it a try.

Sister Léon and mother made a tight body corset with metal plates in the back. I was to wear it day and night. Also, I wasn't to sleep on a pillow; a horror! I believe worst of all was exercising twice a day with a stick behind my elbows. It worked! No surgery. Nobody would guess today that without Sister Léon, my beautiful lady, I might be a hunchback.

Thank you Sister Joseph, thank you Sister Léon.

Faucheur Family

- Marie Bassino Faucheur *(Grand'Mère)* – Auguste Faucheur *(d. 1916)*
  |
- Alice Faucheur *m.* Charles Nourdin *(gassed WWI)*
    Jeannette *(Aunt Alice's daughter from 1st marriage; died of TB, 1941)*
      Louisette *(Jeannette's daughter)*
    Germaine *(Aunt Alice & Charles Nourdin's daughter) m.* Lucien Larrière
      (died of TB)
    Gilbert *(son)*

- Hélène Faucheur *m.* Louis Ququ *(d. 1938)*
    Auguste "Gus" *(sent to German labor, Atlantic Coast)*
    Roger *(joined U.S. Army; KIA Normandy, 1944)*
    Gilberte *(daughter, b. 1928)*

- George Faucheur *(wounded & gassed, WWI; died before WWII)*

- Suzanne Faucheur *m.* Émile Huguin *(Émile spent 3 months in Gestapo
    confinement)*
    Paulette *(daughter)*
    Michel *(son)*

- Thérèse Faucheur *(married; lived further away)*

- Cécile Faucheur *(b. 1909) m.* Marcel Braux *(b. 1902)*
    Nicole Braux *(b. 1927)*

Grandmother Faucheur's Magic Basket

From my first recollection of *Grand'Mère Marie Faucheur* to our last
farewell on my departure for America, I don't remember her ever
visiting us without carrying a basket or sort of satchel—either large,
small, round, or other shape. Of course, the basket's shape wasn't
the important thing, but rather the contents. It always held some gift
for me, something as small as a hard candy, or a little larger, even
a doll. Grandmother's small doll wasn't very showy sitting next to
a magnificent walking doll given to me by St. Nicolas at Christmas

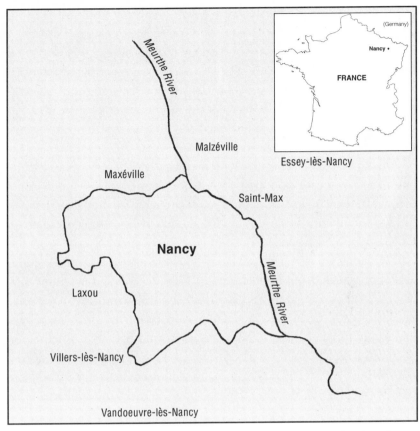

time. The latter type of doll became the craze for young girls after the French government gave them to the English princesses, Elizabeth and Margaret, during a visit. But how I loved the smaller doll grandmother gave me!

Out of grandmother's basket came my first handbag, of white leather. To this day, purses are my weakness for luxury, and a constant remembrance of the joys grandmother provided. Her baskets held affectionate esteem for all. During the economic hard times, it held wonderful things such as pastries, candies, and coins. The money unobtrusively found its way into our cash box, corroborating my father's saying—as long as we had a *sou* (penny) we weren't poor. Often that was all there was in the box before payday. Grandmother, though, often saw to it that it didn't remain there alone.

At the time, six of her ten children were still living, and several had need of the contents in her basket. We always found a pleasant surprise in it. Her generosity knew no bounds, which also extended to her friends, who were numberless. She was a collector. Anything of interest catching her eye went into the basket, either bought or found. A pretty postcard, a scarf, costume jewelry for my mother, always a good cigar for father or her male friends, and things found, such as pieces of string and numerous other objects.

She loved flowers. Our first buttercups and violets always came from her. A parade of vases containing her flowers stood on the window seat of our kitchen. Her love of garden plants probably resulted from her business of growing things for her livelihood after marrying my grandfather, Auguste Faucheur.

Her father (my great grandfather) had been a railroad employee in charge of a small depot in the Laxou suburb of Nancy. I don't know how large her family was. I only met her brother Nicolas and sister Anastasie, but she often spoke of their large family and, being the eldest, she always looked out for her brothers and sisters. Grandmother's own childhood had been difficult, since poverty, disease, and war afflicted France during the 1860s–70s; each day before going to school, she delivered bread for a bakery and picked flowers on the way to sell, in order to supplement the family income.

She told of horrors and starvation in the siege of Nancy by German troops during our nation's disastrous defeat in the Franco-Prussian War, 1870–71. Even rats were hard to find, so hunted they were for food. She told of her fear when hearing *Hulans, Casques à points,* and other names given to the Prussians at the time. She didn't know whether to be more fearful of them or the wolves in the nearby *forêt de Haye* when on her way to Auguste's home in the Marne. Wolves were numerous even near the cities.

She was a gifted storyteller. When spending a night at our house, she shared my bed. I never got enough of her stories. On many occasions, the night passed like an enchantment, but this often angered mother— she felt I was too young for grandmother's adult reminiscences, and colorful language.

Grandmother's way of treating me like a grown-up might've influenced my hunger for reading adult material. In one instance, a neighbor brought over a set of books on World War I, mostly pictures of gory battle scenes and atrocities. Mother didn't want me to see such things, feeling I was too young. Grandmother replied: When would I learn such things? When would I ever be old enough? I looked at the books. Yes, I had terrible nightmares—awake nightmares. But when first meeting my dear Uncle George, a World War I casualty, I was prepared.

Until then, my parents managed to avoid it. Finally, they gave in to my questions about Uncle George. He, too, wanted to visit us and see me—the daughter of his favorite sister. He adored my mother (his baby sister), and she adored him. During World War I, he was wounded over 120 percent of his body—how is that possible? He'd been gassed and lost most of his lungs, lost a leg and arm, and had pieces of shrapnel in his head. He managed to live into his 40s, in and out of hospitals, but most of the time leading a somewhat normal life. He'd married and had a son, but in kindness to his wife, divorced her to give her a chance for leading a more normal life. This I heard about later, after his death.

I recall my first meeting with Uncle George. Grandmother, mother, and I met him in a restaurant for lunch. I can see him to this day. He wore a brown suit and hat. I'd seen many veterans in town with empty sleeves and wooden legs—this was no shock to me. What surprised me was his emotion at meeting me, his niece, for the first time.

I only saw him a few times. Because he couldn't get up flights of stairs, he didn't visit us at home. He spent more and more time at the veterans' hospital. One day, I was told we wouldn't see him anymore. He was gone, but would always be near us, as surely he'd become our guardian angel.

After his death, grandmother changed. She had five daughters, but how could anyone replace her only beloved son who'd suffered so much for so long. Grandmother had lost two baby boys in infancy. Of course, she was sad about that, too, but would say over and again how glad she was they never had to suffer like her son George. I always thought of her as being elderly—of course, a child would. But I noticed a change in her after Uncle George died. She seldom attended mass, but was deeply religious. Now, she'd often go to church alone to pray and beg God to take care of her son.

I never heard enough of my grandmother's talking about the past, of earlier times. Though I only knew grandmother when she was elderly, apparently she was quite beautiful as a young woman. Her daughters (my aunts) often jokingly said: Why don't we look like you?

I asked many times about how she met Grandfather Auguste—such an exciting story to me. She met him at Nancy's fair, held at Cour Léopold—a celebration occurring every August since medieval times. The event's name changed over the years, but for centuries the province fair had been held at the same site.

She was standing near a merry-go-round when a young man offered to ride with her. She accepted. They spent the rest of the afternoon taking all the rides together, met again after that, and soon married. What a romantic story for a youngster like me. She told me what she wore the day they met—a white dress, full of lace and tightly corseted at the waist, the fashion in the 1890s. She also wore a white straw hat with wax cherries, and her feet hurt terribly in white, high, button-up, pointed shoes.

Before she met grandfather, she'd met another man and was very much in love with him. He'd gone to New York to further his studies as a diamond cutter for a jewelry firm. Two or more years went by, then she met my Grandfather Auguste. She no longer had hopes that her first beau would come back. When he eventually returned and was on his way to see her, they met on a tram. By then, however, she'd been married two years and had a child, my Aunt Alice. Such a sad meeting. He returned to New York, but she often spoke of him. Much later, when I planned to marry and go to America, she was my biggest ally against my parents' reluctance. She said I must do it for her—take her place, as she'd made the great mistake of not going.

Grandfather Auguste Faucheur was a poor man. His father and three older brothers were army officers, but he refused to become a professional soldier. As a result, he was disinherited and sent out to make his own way. He and grandmother managed, through much hard work, to buy a vegetable and fruit farm—called *Sainte Elizabeth*—in the wooded hills on the northern outskirts of Nancy near Malzéville. It soon developed, however, that he had little inclination for agricultural labor. A "gentleman farmer" is what he became—with my grandmother doing most of the work. They prospered only through her persistence and stamina, and later with the help of their children.

In 1916, Grandfather Auguste, while reading a newspaper, suddenly died of a stroke. Grandmother kept the farm going until after World War I. Meanwhile, several of her daughters married, and, of course, George returned from the war unable to manage alone. Thus, she moved into Malzéville, living there for the rest of her life.

She was a marvelous mother-in-law to her daughters' husbands. Her son-in-laws loved her and she loved them in return. Her own mother-in-law had been such a good friend to her—she meant to do the same. And she did—a thousand-fold. (My last visit with father occurred in 1977. When he asked if I thought of her, tears swelled in his eyes.)

Grandmother was a most unconventional person—in attitude, speech, dress, and actions. She always wore comfortable but unfashionable black clothes, flat shoes, and heavy wool stockings. According to her, silk stockings were for sissies or street girls. She wore the same type of clothing regardless of the weather—summer or winter. We kept giving her sweaters, but she said they got in her way. During extremely cold snaps, she wore a *pèlerine* (cape)—1910s style—to the great embarrassment of the entire family. I admit to not always being thrilled when being with her in town. I was saddened, though, when one of my cousins crossed the street to avoid being seen with her.

She received respect, love, and affection from people of all walks of life coming in contact with her. Her former servant remained one of her best friends. The priest, aware that she knew everyone in the *paroisse* (parish), asked her for advice on appropriate matters when conducting funerals for deceased local residents. She didn't go to mass often, but regularly supplied flowers for the altar. Malzéville's mayor often asked for her opinions on city matters. A beggar, who seemingly resided on the steps of St. Sébastien church in Nancy, knew her by her first name. Several restaurants reserved a table for grandmother and her "court" of friends.

She was seldom at home, which at times caused concern for the family. Her whereabouts were quite unpredictable. I remember once when my aunts and mother were frantic to find her. It turned out that the police were looking for her, but it was because the chief of police wanted to take her out and visit with her.

Her work involved contacting *jardinières* (fruit and vegetable growers) to place orders for restaurants and grocers, as well as for selling in the city marketplace. Having been a producer herself, she knew everyone within a hundred miles. Not having a telephone, grandmother conducted her transactions directly, constantly keeping her on the move from one part of the countryside to another, checking on the crops herself. She'd promise the delivery of strawberries or other perishables to a restaurant or grocery on a certain day, knowing when these crops would be ready and harvested. She trusted the farmers, and her customers trusted her. Grandmother's visits to the farms provided occasions for parties. With news of her coming, everyone there was invited, or invited themselves, to a feast with wine from the cellars.

She was a marvelous conversationalist, storyteller, and singer, with a repertoire of old songs of which we never tired. She was spellbinding, an enchantment to people of all ages. Almost every Sunday our relatives gathered for dinner at one of my aunts' houses. We seldom met at our small home, however, because of the lack of space. Also, people lived on the floors below us—we needed to be fairly quiet.

When an aunt said, "I am having grandmother for dinner," invariably someone suggested, "Let's make sure we get her to sing!" Other family gatherings occurred for name's days, anniversaries, first communions, or national holidays. Sometimes, a couple of dozen people attended these get-togethers. I enjoyed them tremendously. Grandmother held a gathering each year on her name's day, *Sainte Marie*, the feast of the Assumption—August 15. Being a national holiday, the children could stay up as long as they wished. For the adults—all night was the rule.

The hostess for these gatherings prepared food several days ahead. Each of my aunts had her own specialty that we looked forward to enjoying. Dining began in the early afternoon and lasted until 6 or 7 o'clock in the evening. Sometimes card games followed. During nice weather, we went for walks in the woods or along the Meurthe River, which flows through Malzéville. Some might go to the theatre, ride on merry-go-rounds, play the lotteries, or attend a local dance, and then return for a light supper, enjoying the remnants of the repast.

I preferred grandmother's parties to all the others. She invited many people outside of her family—the priest usually, old friends, and often someone with no family in the locality, usually foreigners. When 10 years old, I met a couple from South America. They were Paraguayan. I was fascinated. She prepared superb meals, but it was her house that proved such a dream to my cousins and me.

Grandmother's very old house on Rue de l'Orme in Malzéville had thick walls, low ceilings, courtyards, and passageways that we weren't sure where they led. We sometimes were a little frightened in the dark areas—or, at least, we enjoyed pretending to be afraid.

Some pieces of furniture dated to the 17th century. Full of her life's memories, the mantle in her living room was covered with photos of people and mementoes of so many kinds. For example, in a beautiful glass "cloche," she kept the orange blossoms from each of her daughter's weddings and many dried flowers from other happy occasions. A beautiful statue of the Virgin Mary stood among these blossoms. Over her bed, there was a painting of the Virgin Mary, illuminated in gold.

Her house contained so many marvelous things to see. She allowed me and my cousins to look in her numerous boxes of souvenirs, as well as her drawers. Of course, she usually allowed us to take some object we'd taken a fancy to.

Once when I was about 6 years old, she took me along to Truveaux, a small village near St. Nicolas. We rode a commuter train, which I enjoyed greatly. Her task on that particular trip was to obtain a large load of *pissenlit* (dandelion greens), which people greatly appreciated as salad greens. We planned to stay for several days, during which time she'd enlist all the available villagers to pick dandelions in the nearby fields.

This was my first journey with her to this place, and I proceeded to shorten her visit due to my actions. The people we stayed with were nice, but my presence was somewhat catastrophic. First, I had to eat all the food heaped on my plate, which included leeks! It was quite an ordeal for me to manage to swallow one. I finally did so, but my greatest ordeal was yet to come.

The Ququ Cousins

Gilberte and her brother Auguste were two of my cousins that I remained closest to throughout the years. During the German occupation, Auguste was sent into construction labor on the French coast. The other son in the Ququ family, Roger, disappeared from Nancy, secretly making his way to North Africa, and eventually signing up with the U.S. Army in Algeria. After the war, an American officer visited the Ququ home with sad word that their vanished son, Roger, died as a tank driver in Normandy. The officer presented Roger's medals to Aunt Hélène.

The farmhouse must've been built around the year 1600 (in my opinion, anyway). Facilities were rudimentary. To take care of my toilet needs, grandmother accompanied me to the "bathroom." It turned out simply to be a latrine somewhere out behind the cows. Not only was I afraid of cows, but I was sure there were cobwebs. Our lantern also created terrible shadows. Quite simply, I needed a proper toilet with a proper seat or there'd be no possible result—instead, only tears, sobs, and a stomach ache.

She took me back to Nancy on the next train—wet panties and all. She was good humored about it. Grandmother's friends had much sympathy and a good laugh. I believe I was 12 years old before I took my next overnight trip with her to the villages.

Her business remained quite prosperous until her health began failing, and World War II began. At first mother assisted her, then took the business over entirely. Grandmother's financial situation then became a worry. The money mother provided for her needs instead often ended up in my pocket, or father's hand, or was spent on a bottle of excellent wine for grandmother's next visit.

My first recollection of Cousin Gilberte (Aunt Hélène and Uncle Louis Ququ's daughter, born in 1928) was at one of the gatherings in grandmother's home. I'm sure we'd seen each other on previous occasions, but this was memorable, since she'd just returned from the hospital after a cataract operation. Cataracts were rare for a youngster. Gilberte still had a bandage over her eyes. I was told to assist her, as she couldn't see. I found it difficult to comprehend someone being unable to see. Afterward, her sight was fine, though she eventually needed reading glasses.

Aunt Hélène gave me a 25-franc silver coin, making me extremely happy—in 1937, a fortune to a 10 year old. The giving meant even more to me when told their family was poor. Her husband, Louis Ququ, worked in a tannery, but earned a small salary. She worked at odd jobs to supplement their income. Grandmother often felt concern for them, and helped a great deal.

The day Aunt Hélène gave me the coin has remained a fond memory. Not just due to the gift, but because of that day's activities. Many of the family had eaten lunch at my Aunt Alice's home. We all decided to enjoy the beautiful spring day by going to the *plateau* and picking *muguet* (lily of the valley) in the woods. On May 1st, it's a French tradition to give a bouquet of *muguet* to loved ones. In the city, one could purchase bouquets from flower sellers, who invaded the sidewalks on these occasions. But if people were fortunate to have access to the

Germaine and Lucien

Aunt Alice was the oldest of the Faucheur children—practically a generation older than my mother, who was born on December 25, 1909. The age difference was such that Aunt Alice's daughter, Germaine, was born six months before my mother was. Being of similar years, Germaine and my mother became as close as sisters when growing up, and married around the same time

Germaine married Lucien Larrière. They were good friends with my parents, since they all were about the same age. Lucien, unfortunately, died of tuberculosis when in his 20s. I retain very fond memories of Lucien. When I was about 7 years old, he already was bedridden. In finding something useful to do, he learned to knit, crochet, and embroider. While Germaine and my mother visited, Lucien taught me to knit, crochet, and make some embroidery stitches. I enjoyed it greatly—to this day I'm a compulsive knitter.

When Lucien died, Germaine had difficulty in making a living and supporting Gilbert, their young son. Her parents took care of Gilbert while she worked.

woods, it provided a marvelous outing for picking your own, which we did that day with great enjoyment.

We left Aunt Alice's house, cousins and all, at about 2 o'clock in the afternoon, strolling up the hill amongst people's gardens. We stopped in Aunt Alice's garden to pick and eat a few strawberries, then proceeded on toward the broad woods and fields of Farm St. Elizabeth, the former Faucheur family home. We decided to go there first before looking for *muguet*. This was my first visit to the house where my grandparents had once lived, and where my mother, aunts, and Uncle George were born. I felt extremely excited. Mother pointed out a path she'd take to school or shop in town. One time, a neighbor's dogs frightened her so much she dropped the groceries she carried, breaking milk bottles. How she'd been punished! Afterward, she walked on another path—longer but less frightening.

Farm St. Elizabeth had been named by earlier owners, perhaps when first built—being hundreds of years old, no one knew the exact date. A statue of St. Elizabeth stood in a niche above the entry door, characteristic of many French houses, even in cities. The farm stood atop a hill, surrounded by woods and meadows. (To my regret, I never had occasion to visit here again before leaving for America.)

To our disappointment, no one seemed home at the time. We'd hoped to visit with the occupants and look inside. We then went into the woods—an enchanting place. We walked and ran all over seeking *muguet*. The scent was indescribable with lilacs in full bloom, also violets, and, of course, magic *muguet*. We picked plenty to take home, as well as wild strawberries, but we children ate them as soon as we found them.

My aunts often came here looking for mushrooms. Other marvelous things grew in these French woods, free for the taking. Once a year in autumn, we gathered blackberry-like *brimbelle*, as well as hazelnuts. When planted in these woods, no one knows. Until after coming to America, I didn't realize these were domesticated plants. I'd always before believed that lilac, for example, was a wild bush.

Later that day, we returned to Aunt Alice's house, put our flowers in water, and enjoyed the treats she always prepared for us, such as *tarte aux mirabelles* (small yellow plums, for which Lorraine is famous), fruits (mainly peaches preserved in alcohol), and garden strawberries in thick cream. Aunt Alice also made a heavenly liquor—children were given only a sip, but if we begged for a second, we usually got it.

Tired, but so contented, we returned home on the tram, similar in appearance to San Francisco's well-known cable cars. The clanking and ringing of tramway cars were as much a part of daily life as the sound of church bells.

La Fête au Village

Not quite comparable to American county fairs, but with some similarities, the *fête* has been a part of French life since time immemorial. Nancy's *fête* was large, of course, and lasted two weeks, following a preceding two-week industrial arts exposition. We attended many times, especially on fireworks night.

Going to Malzéville's fair, however, was more of a tradition in our family, probably because more of our relatives lived in that neighborhood. What excitement for a little girl. The expectations! I'd save money for weeks to pay for rides and try my luck at the games. After getting off the tram and nearing a bridge, the sounds of the *Fête de Malzéville* first came to our ears—a cacophony of merry-go-round music, Viennese waltzes, popular songs, and possibly the national anthem, the *Marseillaise*, or other patriotic tunes performed by the Malzéville band. Once I remember hearing the small, circular-shaped, Swiss trumpet, the *Cour de Chasse*, being played. There also was much singing in the *brasseries* (coffee shops/restaurants).

Next came the smell of *gaufres* (waffles), *frites* (French fries), and sauces, making our mouths water. Then a riot of bright colors, with red and gold prominent and all providing pleasure to the eye. Our parents tried to keep us together, but soon my cousins, our friends, and I were running everywhere, discovering all sorts of delights. *Les petites chaise* was my favorite ride—little seats attached to long chains that fanned out when picking up speed. I'm told they were dangerous, but in those days no one thought of that.

Exhausted, dizzy, and dusty after several hours of indescribable fun, we gathered at Aunt Alice's for dinner, then returned. This was more the time for grownups, with the *Bal des Jardinières* (Gardeners' Ball) held in Malzéville's music hall, the Printania. While street dancing occurred everywhere, the *Grand Bal* was held at the Printania.

My mother and father—Cécile Faucheur and Marcel Braux—first met at one of these balls. Loving to dance and being exceptional at it, father attended many balls when a young man. After meeting mother, here are the words he later wrote from Savigny—

Chère Amie,

Je vous envoie deux mots comme je vous l'ai promis.

Je n'ais pas grand chose a vous apprendre, depuis que nous nous somme quittés.

Je suis rentree en bon port et j'espère qu'il en est de meme pour vous.

Je suis impatient de vous revoir, soyez certain que si je vais vous voir au Printania ce n'est pas en desinteresse et je serais heureux de faire connaissance avec vôtre mère.

Ne vous meprenez pas sur ce que je vous avoue, mais vous m'avez fait une grande impression de la verité. Je ne vous écrit pas plus longuement pour cette fois, mais j'espère que vous m'écrirez aussi en attendant de vous revoir le 3 Octobre.

Un ami qui peuse souvent a vous depuis le jour qu'it vous à recontre et qui vous aime.

Marcel Braux

In English:

Dear Friend,

I am writing to you as I have promised I would.

I have little news to add since I have last seen you.

I had a good journey back and I hope the same is true for you.

I am anxious to see you again. Be sure that when I return to see you at the Printania it is with the best of intentions, and I will be glad to call on your mother.

Do not misunderstand my interest, but you gave me the sweet impression of the trust and hope that you will also write to me before we meet again, October 3rd.

A friend who thinks of you since the day that we first met and who loves you.

Marcel Braux

The letter is very precious to me. Father did meet grandmother. With her approval, they returned to the dances; mother and father married the following January, 1926.

Communion Solennelle (First Communion)

Children were baptized when a few days old—an occasion for a family reunion and celebration. We little ones, of course, could hardly participate consciously—we were lucky if we received our milk feeding during these festivities.

A *Communion Privé* was conducted at 7 or 8 years of age. But our *Communion Solennelle*—at the age of 11 or 12—was our greatest moment as "almost adults" before marriage. By now we lived on Blvd. Foch in Laxou, my home throughout the war years.

After a year of preparation in catechism, we formally joined the church in the first communion, followed a few days later with confirmation by the bishop. These were happy times for me—at least in church. At home, it was a tormented period because of the approaching war—of this I will say much more later. Now I will speak of happy times, only marred by a few moments of anguish as occurs in youth. I felt the joys at church were truly wonderful. I'd anticipated this day for a long time—to wear a long white dress and trailing veil for the magnificent ceremony to come—truly becoming a child of God.

One thing cast a shadow over my joy. I'd be wearing a borrowed dress, as my family felt it unnecessary to buy a costly new one. To this day, I've been saddened by returning the dress. I so wish I could've kept it—to look at it, and show it to my children. The meaning of the ceremony didn't depend on the clothing (I know that now), but it was difficult for a child of 12 to accept.

As customary, a large family reunion would be held at the time of my first communion, with a glorious table of food, and champagne—I could drink a glass on that day. A happy time, never to be forgotten. I'll say more about this later.

Cousin Gilberte's first communion, occurring a year after mine, also was memorable. Being 13 years old, I began noticing boys. I'd developed a crush on her brother, Roger. It didn't last long. Another cousin,

Braux Family Neighbors, Blvd. Foch Locality, Laxou

The Brauxs occupied 3rd (top) floor of house

- Pierre *(Italian)* & Marguerite *(French)* Guissiani – *occupied 1st floor*
        (Mr. Guissiani spent 6 months in Gestapo confinement)
    Pierre "Pierrot" *(son; disappeared & joined Maquis, FFI)*
    Micheline *(daughter)*
    Jean "Jeannot" *(son)*
    Gerard *(baby son)*

- Fernand & Madeleine Kronemaker – *occupied 2nd floor*
- Mr. & Mrs. Pinnel – *lived two houses away (Mrs. Pinnel, Jewish, seized by*
        Gestapo; died a few months after returning)
    Jacques *(Jacques & father not taken by Gestapo)*
    Daughter *(husband in POW camp)*

- Mr. Zint *(age about 60)* & Mrs. Zint – *resided next door, 1st floor*
    Huguette *(daughter)*
    Jean *(son; Merchant Marine; joined Free French forces)*

- Guy Calba *(20 years old, 1944; FFI member)*
- Jean Dehant *(Calba's friend, 1944; FFI member)*
- Lucette Fouillouse *(20 years old, 1944)*
- Gildo *(Italian; same age as Nicole)*
- Jean *(neighborhood youth; killed by land mine)*
- Yvonne Roth *(20 years old, 1944)*

Others in the Nancy area—

- Mrs. Marcelle & Mr. Bérin – *lived in Aunt Suzanne's Essey neighborhood*
        (Mr. Bérin in Résistance; disappeared in Gestapo hands)
    Raymond *(son; joined Résistance)*
    Suzanne *(daughter)*
- Denise Bredin *(about Nicole's age)*
- Mr. Cadario *(Italian; Guissiani's relative; architect & builder; shot by Germans)*
- René Lunot *(police chief; apparent collaborator; secretly a Résistance*
        leader)
- Odette Mangeot *(lived in Aunt Suzanne's Essey neighborhood)*
- Nadine *(married Pierrot Guissiani after the war)*
- Mr. Piquemale *(Spanish; citrus produce wholesaler)*
- Mr. Roux *(music teacher)*
- Walty *(Cousin Paulette's German friend; later died on Russian Front)*

Paulette, told me forthwith that one doesn't fall in love with one's cousin. Nevertheless, it made that reunion very exciting for me.

I also accompanied mother to the communion for one of her friend's sons, conducted in a small town church outside of Nancy. The local *fête au village* coincided, giving us the opportunity to enjoy rides almost all evening long in the village square. We spent the night in an old mill remodeled into a home. We hardly slept, due to the still-operable waterwheel clanking and squeaking alongside one wall of the house, as well as the churning babble of the small river.

Grandmother and her brother Nicholas sang duets, delighting everyone. Someone brought along an accordion for accompaniment. The old French songs, full of romance and tragedy, moved us so much. But when they ended their sets with *Le Madelon* or one of Maurice Chevalier's latest songs, our tears dried quickly and everyone joined in. Though exhausted when returning home, we had such good memories to treasure.

The Depression

When playing at home during those years, I learned a little of what the Depression was all about. I enjoyed pretending to be a jeweler—sanding wood for father as he made a few luxury wooden pieces for selling to friends. I'd pick up nails and pins for mother as she sewed fur clothing. But for them it was hard, tiring, tedious work, just to make a little extra money.

Some comments they made are understandable to me today, such as Grandmother Braux's grumbling about having to knit socks when she was a "lace maker!" To me, those socks seemed every bit as much fun to make as fine lace work, and so much faster to accomplish. The fur jobs that mother completed appeared like miracles to me, but she complained of soreness after doing this work. How could this be after making a fox stole with a marvelous little *gutta-percha* (resin) covered head, looking so real I knew this fox could smell again, and the glass eyes surely watched me. She even made a tiger-like rug, with a head looking so real and ready to bite that I was afraid of it.

Why did father sound sad, but also happy, when saying he couldn't believe he was wrapping candies in *roudoudou* (small decorative wooden containers)? I now realize it was terribly demeaning for him to do such tasks to add to his income at the confectionary firm, where he worked as an inventory and distribution clerk. He was ever so pleased when mother's pay topped his, even though his pride was hurt.

I remember the day well—mother waltzed in with good things to eat and drink, and flowers, to celebrate her big raise at Gasser's, who were friends with grandmother. At Gasser's, mother had learned the furrier trade; though left-handed, she managed to operate the specialized right-handed fur sewing machine. It was a payday—not checks in those days, but cash in an envelope. She put it on the table. Father came in, putting his envelope down. Mother, in her joy, spread her bills out. Father didn't open his. But his sadness soon dissipated, and we had a lovely celebration. He complained about his boss, and congratulated my mother.

In my youth, I didn't know what it meant for Grandmother Braux to visit the bakery shop early Monday mornings, buying Sunday's leftover bread and pastries at half price. She feared meeting friends and being "dishonored." Of course, many of them probably did just the same thing, but none dared mentioning it. If meeting someone she knew, grandmother said she'd claim to have forgotten to pick up an order on Sunday, or that we were gone on the weekend and weren't able to get to the shop.

We didn't lack all that many necessities (after all, day-old pastry is sufficient food), but still, the Depression was difficult for most everyone, shattering self-respect in small and large ways. Father cried when making out an application for Social Insurance when mother became ill and couldn't work. It was insulting to him, being unable to pay the doctor and pharmacist bills. These programs were new to the French in the 1930s, and often difficult for a Frenchman's pride. Yet, Social Insurance proved a godsend to us at that particularly difficult time. Being too young to encompass such things, I was unaware of the full economic adversity impacting the nation.

War Clouds Gather

People were accustomed to foreigners moving to France, escaping social, economic, and political difficulties in their own countries. Mr. Piquemale, a local resident, fled upheaval and military conflict in Spain (along with many thousands of his countrymen), coming to France a few years previously. Many Italians such as Pierre Guissiani, our neighbor on Blvd. Foch, also left their country, which the Depression affected even worse than France. These people largely came to find work. Most did, and now were established and integrated. They raised families and hardly anyone thought of them as foreigners.

The newest refugees, however, were different. It was disturbing. They were frightened and told stories no one dared or wanted to believe. Most were Jews from Germany and Central Europe, coming with only their clothes and practically nothing else. Many really didn't want to remain in Lorraine, so close to Germany. They were on their way to Paris or the south—even to England.

One group of traveling Gypsies remained for the winter instead of moving on as usual, making me quite happy. They camped in a field only a block away. We greatly enjoyed their entertainments—a small circus, dancing in costume, and marvelous music. They arrived during the first summer when we moved to Blvd. Foch. My friends and I frequently visited the camp.

I befriended one of the girls, Santina, who was about my age—companions at first sight. She invited me into their *roulotte* (wagon). I was surprised to see a modern, if small, kitchen with refrigerator, but also felt a little disappointed in not finding something more exotic. I loved their clothing and, most of all, the language. This again revealed my respect for foreign peoples about whom I had an insatiable curiosity.

I was so happy to see her again in the following summer. So were my girlfriends. Santina had several brothers, one absolutely "beautiful." Since I was his sister's friend, he gave me tickets for as many rides as I wanted to take. A truly wonderful summer. At the coming of spring, they left, not home to Romania, but to southern France. They weren't allowed to cross Germany. People didn't or wished not to believe their stories about persecution. There is a saying—*histoires de Romanichels* ("Gypsies' tales"). We learned much later that it was true; Gypsies were sent into concentration camps, same as the Jews. I never saw Santina again. I hope they secretly made their home in unoccupied (Vichy) France or the Italian sectors during the war, as did many Jews, too, and didn't get rounded up by the Nazis.

Father read *Match* every week. I usually didn't pay much attention to this magazine, it being so boring to a young person. But one issue of *Match* remains vivid in my memory. As father sat reading on a Sunday afternoon, he called mother and they had a discussion. They were in consternation, and appalled. I became curious, so father showed the magazine to me and talked about what Adolf Hitler and the Nazi Party could mean for us. I tried to visualize this as a reality, as adults did. Father spent much time discussing this with me that day.

He believed war was imminent. According to his military classification, he'd be in the first group mobilized. He expected to be called up soon. Yes, everyone thought he was a pessimist. I thought so, too, but he was earnest. I listened carefully, but pretty much as if only hearing a story. Looking back, I realize I started becoming an adult that day, or at least joined grownups in an increasing concern about an uncertain, frightening future. From that day on, war wasn't just stories, epics, and hero tales for me, but pain, sorrow, and the fear of tomorrow. Father's pessimism proved correct. In March 1939, Hitler occupied all of Czéchoslovakia, contrary to international agreement.

Our doorbell rang at about 10 p.m. We looked at each other, knowing what it meant. A sergeant had come with father's recall papers; they gave him two hours to get ready. He dressed in his reserve uniform, packed a bag, and kissed and hugged us with all his might. This was just before my first communion, to be held in May; father promised to come back, even

"Father"—Marcel Braux, before leaving for the war.

if he had to go AWOL (Absent without Leave). Mother and I cried for much of the night.

Father was assigned not far west at Foug, near Toul, where his "Genie" outfit was stationed. The following Sunday, we went by train to visit him, bringing cake and other things. Mother asked where he could be found and to our dismay was told, "In the brig." Horror, what'd he done?

When entering a large dormitory, our fears dissipated—he was playing cards. The wives or fiancées of several other men also were visiting and no one appeared unhappy. Father and the other soldiers were detained because they'd tried to go home on Saturday. With no assigned duty for the weekend, they assumed they could leave, but it wasn't so. They were stopped at the railroad station, brought back, and restricted to the barracks.

This military call-up turned out to be short-lived, as tensions with Germany lessened somewhat. In a few weeks, the demobilized reserves came home. There was joy all around—everything would be alright! But father said not to rejoice too soon. They'd been briefed—if recalled again, expect it to be for good.

In the meantime, happy with father at home, I looked forward to my first communion and taking exams to earn a *certificat d'études*. I studied and prepared as best I could. The exams were held at the École Émile Gebhart, which seemed a good omen as this was the first school I'd attended. For two days, we were tested in various fields. An hour after the final exam, the students' names and placements were to be posted outside by the door. With 2,000 students taking the tests, many anxious parents and their children waited on the sidewalk—really like a mob.

It took me a long time to get close enough to see the posting, finding my way among impatient, jubilant, and broken-hearted students and parents. On the list, a red line divided the accepted above from the rejected below. I wasn't sure where to look first. But feeling good about my exams, I decided to look at the top part. I'd passed, at 75th on the list! I was out of my mind with joy, but soon even more so. When walking across the street to take the news home—lo, there stood father

"École Émile Gebhart—boys attended classes in the forefront section, and girls in the nearly identical portion to the left."

grinning from ear to ear and leaning on the most magnificent, new, pale-green, Peugeot bicycle I'd ever seen.

He hugged me, saying the bicycle was mine.

"But," I said, "how'd you know I'd pass?"

He said he hadn't any doubt about it.

We walked home, both of us pushing the bike. Mother had prepared a fine dinner. A happy day. Of course, they had to sit through my detailed descriptions of the exams—all the questions and answers I could recall. It was great fun—one of those days isolated from the current world trends where tomorrow only existed in a fleeting cloud of hope. When feeling so good, how could one not feel that tomorrow would be just as glorious? School continued for a few weeks, but students who'd passed the exams weren't obligated to attend. I missed some days.

School ended—joy! I had my *certificat d'études* and felt like celebrating. An outdoor ball was organized for the students, with games, food, drink, and dancing. We held contests in the afternoon. Knowing I couldn't win the beauty contest, I signed up for the ugliness one instead, consisting of making faces. Lo, I won first prize! It wasn't too flattering and I'm sure I wasn't terribly happy about it, but I was a good sport. I won a toy sailboat, which I gave to a younger neighbor friend, Jeannot Guissiani.

The picnic was held in the evening, then the long-anticipated dance. This was a special joy as I could show off my father. Sure enough, not long after the dancing began, people started giving him room on the dance floor. Everyone stopped to watch him and his partner, a woman I didn't know, then people began clapping and asking them to keep going. I felt so proud. (After the war, he taught dancing for awhile. I was living in America by then, but wish I could've seen him.)

During all this enjoyment, I began feeling unwell. As I came home, I realized something important was happening—I'd become a woman. I shouted this to father. He told mother, and we had another celebration. I think I became somewhat tipsy for the first time in my life.

It was glorious to forget about school things and concentrate on preparations for my communion. This was even more important to me than the *certificat d'études*. This time, no fallible teachers would be giving exams; God would be testing me. I plunged into it with all my heart. The perfect day arrived. No words can describe the ecstasy in the life of a 12-year-old. Even the streets looked magnificent with so many communicants walking toward the church—about 30 girls, all in white with long veils floating in the breeze, and about the same number of boys in black suits. We were truly like angels floating toward a great moment in our lives.

The ringing of the bells drew us along with the promise of joy surrounding us. Outside the church, the nuns organized us into ranks. When the priest gave the signal, the procession entered the church led by the sacristan in his gala uniform and the altar boy dressed in lace and carrying a beautiful banner. We followed, taking our places—girls on the right, boys to the left. It was the most beautiful day in our religious lives.

After the ceremony, we returned home for lunch—with great appreciation, since we hadn't eaten since the previous day. At 3 p.m., we

"My first communion, 12 years old."

returned to vesper service dedicated to the Virgin Mary. I had a good voice and often sang in the choir. For this service, six of us were chosen to sing by the *Ste. Thérèse* chapel in the church. I was scared, but so glad to be selected. That evening, relatives came over for dinner. It was a very happy party. Grandmother Faucheur sang, of course, and I was being sent off toward my adult life.

As was customary, the day after communion and dressed in the white dress and veil, I visited my master teacher, Madame Étienne. It was pleasant to do so, though probably tiring for her with all the 12 year olds having communion at the same time. One student, being Protestant, was excluded from these festivities. She actually was the only Protestant I knew. Her communion would occur when she became 15. I had little knowledge of Protestantism at the time, in fact, practically none at all, except that they didn't want anything to do with our church. On the other hand, I knew quite a lot about the Jewish faith, though Jews probably were small in number, only having one large synagogue standing amongst 30 or so Catholic churches in Nancy.

Two weeks later, we repeated our vows as *Catholiques* at Notre Dame de Bonsecour, one of the oldest churches in Nancy. That same day, we joyfully attended the St. Nicolas church for our confirmation by the bishop. After I approached the bishop and told him my name, he said I'd be surrounded by children all my life—they'd be my happiness. He spoke rightly. It's always been so. As a mother and teacher, I've been blessed with their presence in my life.

This was a busy, exciting time in my young life. Days never had enough hours. But also, I felt like I was on an emotional roller coaster, going from moments of ecstasy and joy, to extremes of despondency at other times.

Tocsin

In France, *tocsin* means the ringing of church bells to announce the outbreak of war. People who'd lived through the First World War knew this sound; only the young hadn't heard it. It took only a few peals of the bells, however, to understand the meaning.

With school and communion over, I was on summer vacation. It'd started marvelously. Father took me out every evening, teaching me how to ride my bike. How patient he was when walking alongside as I clumsily tried to sit straight and keep my feet on the pedals. Then he'd run alongside me. When finally running too fast for his liking, he said I was ready to go out alone.

I began riding with friends—the happiest girl in the neighborhood. Mother knew how to ride and I loaned her my bicycle now and then. She'd owned one when a young girl, paying for it with her own money by tending a goat and selling the milk to neighbors. She recalled many stories about this fantastic clothes-eating and vegetable-gobbling goat! It caused mother many problems, but she got her bicycle, with the first money she'd earned. She often reminisced about this period of her life.

Bike riding provided new freedom, even though my parents put restrictions on where I could go. I obeyed, no matter how strongly friends coaxed me to ride elsewhere, especially to meet boys in other neighborhoods. For the time being, the boys on our street were quite sufficient as I was still too young to care much. I couldn't understand my older friends' wanderlust, thinking them "loose women." They wore lipstick and other wicked adornments I swore to never use. Time would soon change me, of course.

The summer of 1939 was lovely, if one didn't listen too much to adult conversation. War fears constantly reminded us that all wasn't well in the world. Young people avoided adult company in order to enjoy these last months of unmarred pleasures. I played cards with the boys. They even allowed me to join them in soccer, without my parents' knowledge, of course. I had difficulty explaining my bruises, using bicycling as an excuse, saying I'd fallen.

Pierre Guissiani, our Italian neighbor with a growing family, worked as a contractor for his older relative, Mr. Cadario, an architect who had built row houses in a "modern" style (including ours) in this part of town. Thus, Mr. Guissiani had access to building materials and tools. The Guissiani family lived on the 1st floor of our building, the Kronemakers on the 2nd floor, and we occupied the 3rd (top) floor. Mr. Guissiani and father put their heads and efforts together to prepare a bomb shelter in our building's basement. This brought physical evidence of the adults' fears. It was difficult to ignore; their concern for the future wasn't just talk, but a factual thing. Of course, we children enjoyed playing around the project. Many neighbors, though, laughed at them. These people still said, "The Germans would never dare attack France."

But they kept on building the shelter. Mr. Guissiani had left Italy knowing Mussolini's fascist government lied when claiming no one there could go hungry. Father could read between the lines of newspaper accounts claiming France stood safe behind the Maginot Line. Father believed the Maginot Line was outmoded, a hoax. He'd seen these massive border fortifications during his short army duty in the spring. His outfit was briefed on what to do in case of war, as they'd be stationed there.

The French government's requisitioning of cars and trucks was another indicator hard to ignore. As people brought them in, the vehicles were parked in a nearby field, where we children played soccer and rolled in the grass. Only doctors or people absolutely needing vehicles for their work were allowed to keep them.

Signs of impending disaster now sprang up constantly in news reports, building to a climax in late August. Father, aware he'd be among the first group recalled, was serious when talking to mother about making future preparations and the need for caution during his possibly long absence. People remembered the atrocities committed by German troops during their occupation of Lorraine in World War I. Everyone feared an imminent renewal of this danger. Father told us how to prepare. He was terribly frightened over our fate, knowing he wouldn't be home to protect us against the eventualities of war. For a youngster, of course, it now was becoming difficult to maintain the exhilaration of youthful pleasures in such threatening times.

When father had been called up in March, he'd promised to return for my communion. Though pessimistic about the international situation then, he knew he'd be back. When now recalled and leaving us in late August, the farewell was terribly sad. He knew he'd be absent a long time, made no promises, and acted despondent when leaving us. It was one of the saddest days of our lives, knowing this was the catastrophe we'd tried so hard to push out of our minds in carrying on daily life. Father left on a Tuesday. Everyday, more men were called up in the general mobilization.

On September 1, after Sunday lunch, I walked to the Sarnal grocery, three blocks from home. When coming back, I heard the church bells. From the mournful, evenly spaced ringing, everyone knew we were at war. Germany had attacked Poland! I ran home, passing by silent, stunned people standing helplessly on their porches or sidewalks. I found mother at Mrs. Guissiani's, as well as Mrs. Kronemaker, the lady from the 2nd floor apartment whose husband worked for the railroad. They were crying, and so sad—the beginning of life as women without men.

Mr. Guissiani, not being a French citizen, wasn't required to enlist in the reserves, but joined after father left. Even though the Guissianis had three children, and expected a fourth, Pierre signed up, feeling as patriotic as if he'd been born French. At this time, Italians weren't greatly loved because of Mussolini. Italian expatriates, however, were truly anti-fascists. They wished to resist dictatorships even more strongly than many of the French born. I'd vocally rise in their defense many times during our ugly war.

Grandmother Braux, in shock over her son leaving for the front, was inconsolable, mostly remaining a recluse in her room in our apartment or at church. Her health, already not good, deteriorated further. We were helpless in providing encouragement and so unhappy ourselves.

Mother now would have to force aside her own sorrow and work longer hours, making up for father's lost salary. The government supposedly granted a monetary allowance, but no one knew how much, or when it would arrive. Despite our sadness, we needed to survive, and mother had no alternative. We required additional money to purchase food and necessities for the eventual shortages of wartime.

Early Monday morning, September 2, I joined a large crowd in front of the local grocery store, waiting for the doors to open. Everyone jealously guarded their place in line, making sure the latest arriving people didn't get ahead. The queue was somewhat disorganized, and we were shy and embarrassed. This was the first of thousands of queues we'd be standing in during the war. We would learn quickly, becoming efficient in this miserable game—spending every spare moment standing in line or planning out which shops to visit next in hopes of finding a scrap of food or pair of socks.

In a short while, the sidewalk in front of the grocery filled with people. I waited until 11 a.m. for my turn to go inside. Seeing the large bags people carried out, I didn't think it possible there'd be anything left. Being only 12 years old, I didn't quite understand why people were doing this—buying sugar, flour, and salt in large kilo packs. Prices soared by the hour. When my turn came, I spent all the money I had with me. Being a child, I bought what I liked—chocolate, sardines, tuna, cookies, and such things. Since I needed to move fast, I gathered up a lot of a few things, and somehow managed to carry it all home.

Mother was astounded at the pile of chocolate bars and extremely unhappy with the purchases. Nevertheless, as the years went by, these proved to be a treasure beyond compare when such items no longer were available. How we later laughed at my first effort in "queuing."

But how tragic—people already hoarding food and supplies on only the second day of the war. By mid-afternoon, the grocery's shelves stood empty, a grim omen for the future. They'd doubled, even quadrupled, prices as the hours passed, but this hadn't deterred anyone who'd stood in line. People feared, with good foresight, that food transportation would be restricted or even stopped. The government already had requisitioned most cars, trucks, and trains. Essential roadways were restricted to only military use. Consequently, secondary roads became congested with civilians trying to reach other towns or rejoin families.

Stories of eating rats in previous wars resurfaced in peoples' thoughts. Grandmother Faucheur often told us about this in the 1870 war. No longer a tale to me, it now was a real possibility.

Looking back, I believe that people—otherwise feeling so helpless and overwhelmed by events—adopted this frantic purchasing activity as a means of coping. It was a tangible thing they could do in protecting their families. But the foremost fear, of course, was what to expect in regard to the Germans. We listened to every report of Poland's continuing collapse, and shuddered. Mothers—alone at home caring for children and fearing their husbands' fates—felt extremely apprehensive; children were kept inside.

The civilian working sector came to a standstill—factories, offices, banks, practically everything, closed. New workers would be needed with so many men leaving within a few days. Women would soon go to work, making up for the absence of their husbands' salaries. It proved extremely difficult for women who'd never worked before and had no training or preparation. They also faced difficulties in finding care for their children. Many fell into a state of panic over these troubling changes.

The first week of the war ended my childhood, as if a fairy touched me with a magic wand. My mother, a shy and gentle woman, clung to me as much as I did to her. Grandmother Faucheur was our savior; she mustered us to action. She said mother could work for her in the produce business until the furriers reopened their doors. I'd keep house until school started in October. Grandmother had survived two wars—a third was simply matter of fact. We might not survive, but in the meantime we'd keep going. She repeated many clichés, but everything was clichés during those times, and we needed to end our lethargy.

Little by little, life returned to a somewhat usual pace. The post offices reopened, with women and older men serving as mail carriers. Tramway and train service resumed, and banks, offices, and businesses reopened. This return to normalcy gave us a somewhat brighter outlook. We began circulating in the community again, visiting relatives and friends. I missed father terribly, but almost all my friends were in the same situation, so it became a way of life. We lived day by day, wondering what the next would bring. Since young people usually are more optimistic, perhaps we initially were more resilient. Tomorrow seemed less frightening to us than for the adults, but this soon changed as our lives drastically altered.

Gasmasks

Gasmasks were issued shortly after the declaration of war. The masks were carried in a holder, suspended by a belt-like strap arrangement attached from the shoulder. They included drab grey-green canisters about 20 inches long by 8 inches in diameter. A novelty in the beginning and even fun for youngsters to play with, they became a great nuisance after awhile. It wasn't long before they wound up in many people's closets.

Everyone, of course, feared a German gas attack. After World War I's ghastly results, we all felt dread. Two of my uncles, George and Charles, had suffered gas inflicted injuries.

We young people, however, had lots of fun with our masks. Later on, after school started again, we enjoyed a kind of race with them. Rue Pierre Curie was on a fairly steep hill. At the top of this street, we'd line up our masks in a row, someone then gave a signal, and we'd give them a kick. They rolled downhill with a clatter. This damaged them somewhat, but we weren't too concerned.

We eventually tired of this game, but still had to carry them to school or receive demerit points. Of course, the teachers didn't take the time to check inside the containers. They might've been surprised to find smuggled food, books, and toys. With so little enjoyment to be had, we made the most of anything at hand.

Food Coupons

With France on a wartime footing, food shortages developed. The government controlled and equalized distribution by issuing *tickets* (coupons), restricting each person to a proscribed amount of provisions per day. It began with coupons required for the purchase of bread, then meat, and later on to everything from toothpaste to bobby pins. Nearly all food and clothing eventually were rationed. Most everyone I knew planted gardens.

Initially, everyone complained bitterly, but we would've rejoiced at that time if we'd known what was yet to come. What, just "one" cream puff or croissant per person after waiting half an hour for our turn at the *pâtisserie*! A year later, we'd be fortunate to get half of a moldy, brown, doughy *baguette* after hours of queuing!

Obtaining the coupons proved problematic. They were distributed at the city hall. If family members were at work or school, one of them needed to take the day off and queue for hours. At first, Grandmother Braux picked ours up. But as her legs bothered her more and more, either mother or I had to go. It was a problem for many people. The administration wasn't prepared for such an eventuality; it was chaos.

Cities suffered the most due to the shortage of train service, on which France relied heavily for food transport. Milk remained in great scarcity because it came from farms outside of urban areas. After our troops fully moved into positions in the Maginot Line, this problem eased somewhat.

First Bombing

At about 7 o'clock one morning, we heard our first air raid alarm of the war. What pandemonium! I later was told that our neighbor, Mr. Zint, initially came out onto the sidewalk wearing only a shirt. Afterwards, some claimed they'd seen "everything"—at Mr. Zint's expense, we needed a laugh.

As the air raid began, people said we should go with Mr. Zint and his family to their garden shed about 200 yards up the hill. They felt our basement shelter would be a tomb if the building fell on us; we'd be buried by rubble.

We followed Mr. Zint. Many people fled to these family garden plots and sheds. Everyone felt panic, especially when first hearing and spotting the German planes. They flew low near our neighborhood. I don't recall how many—four, five, maybe six. We quietly huddled, listening. Two bombs exploded nearby. The raid lasted a few minutes, then silence. Shortly, we heard the long wail of the all-clear signal, indicating the end of the raid. We cautiously looked out, then we returned home, anxious to know where the bombs fell and if there were victims. We no longer were quite as cocky as earlier when nothing had yet happened to us in this war.

A little later that morning, we heard that bombs fell around the Charlemagne school, about four blocks away. We were shocked! Nine people heading for the shelter were killed near the door, our mailman

"The Charlemagne school, which I attended for a time."

among them. He'd paused to let a woman go in ahead of him—she wasn't even scratched.

We were aghast—war had begun for us!

From then on, alerts sounded every night, periodically even two or three times. Sometimes bombing followed, other times the planes passed overhead to other destinations. The Germans didn't seem to usually have particular targets in mind—only dropping a few bombs at random. This was harassment, meant to demoralize and disrupt our lives—people would be exhausted at work after being up all night.

We feared using our basement shelter after hearing about victims buried in collapsed buildings. Mrs. Guissiani said we could make use of an almost furnished villa outside of town. The prospective owners had left the area, and the house—at least for the present—currently belonged to her husband's relative, the architect Mr. Cadario. We took mattresses, blankets, and a few necessities, including food and drink. Every evening at nightfall, we'd walk about three miles to the villa to spend the night. We slept soundly the first few nights, so thankful of our good fortune. Feeling so safe, we didn't pay much attention to the air raid alarms.

It was a pleasant walk, taking *sentiers* (paths) among peoples' gardens as shortcuts. One moonlit night, Mrs. Guissiani's son, Pierrot, was kind of sweet toward me, not a rough pal as usual. He told me to stay close to him in case we had problems—he'd watch over me, and besides, he said, I was becoming pretty.

We all stayed close by him. Pierrot was just a little older than me, but the only male in our group aside from Mr. Zint, who was about 60 years old, overweight, rheumatic, and afraid of his own shadow. I carried Pierrot's little brother, Jeannot. He wouldn't go with anyone but me; he even slept with me. Pierrot carried his sister Micheline, who was afraid to walk in the dark. She also slept with me. We were terribly crowded on our little mattress.

After getting good sleep for several nights, the exhilaration in going to our refuge gradually wore off and the nightly trek became less enjoyable. We wondered how long we could keep it up. Grandmother Braux started asking us to leave her at home because her legs felt so bad. She didn't care if she died in the bombing. People, too, were beginning to get on each other's nerves. Coughing, snoring, and such were becoming unbearable, and we felt concern over the coming bad weather. One day was quite difficult, with the paths muddy after a rain. Well, we'd see—we lived day by day.

The decision was made for us one night. As the air raid alert sounded, some listened a bit, some continued sleeping. We heard planes coming near, but weren't fearful. As far as we knew, there wasn't anything to bomb in the villa's locality where only a few scattered houses stood hidden by trees. Nearby was Parc de Brabois—the race course and velodrome where car and motorcycle races were held. I'd gone there many times before the war. Nothing to attack there. But the planes came closer and closer, then bombs began dropping on the velodrome! We dared not move. In a few minutes it was over, and daylight approached. We silently prepared to leave.

Before turning toward home, we walked up the hill a short distance to see where the bombs fell. We discovered the target! A large group of French tanks stood parked in the velodrome. We hadn't seen them from the house because our view was blocked off. A few looked damaged, but we supposed their fuel tanks were empty since they didn't catch fire. We were astounded!

We'd felt so safe! From now on, we'd simply stay home and keep on praying. It'd worked before, hadn't it? This was our family's decision, as it was for everyone from then on.

After a while, the German planes came less and less. During an alert, we sometimes went to the basement and sometimes not. Grandmother Braux's condition worsened. If we took her to the shelter, we had to carry her all the way down, and then back up all those long flights of stairs.

At school it was much the same. In the beginning, we'd all go to the shelter during daytime alerts. It was mayhem with several hundred children packed in like sardines. After a while when getting accustomed to air raids, teachers sent out a reliable student to listen for planes. If they approached closely, the student blew a whistle and we'd go to the shelter.

Actually, Nancy suffered little during these months. Only a handful of people were killed or wounded, and the damage was minimal. For a long period, we weren't much bothered. We relaxed and hoped this was all. Perhaps the war would end soon. There was talk about it being over by winter, with Hitler giving in and our men returning home.

Grandmother Braux

Grand'Mère, Grand'Mère—I'd hardly spent a day since I was born without being near my Grandmother Braux. Mother wrote to father about our difficulties, including the fact that grandmother could hardly walk or leave her bed, so we didn't take her down to the bomb shelter. We feared for the future—if the war escalated, how could we care for her? I attended school and mother worked all day. We were at an impasse. If he agreed, grandmother was willing to go to Lay St. Christophe, a home for the elderly run by a Catholic organization. He thought this was best. He was so sad not to be with us in these times. Now on the Maginot Line, he didn't even get out for fresh air.

The day my grandmother left was terribly sad. She dressed in the somewhat old-fashioned clothes ladies her age preferred—her best long black skirt and a black blouse with small white collar. I'll always remember her looking around the apartment for the last time. Of course, we told her that she'd be back as soon as the war ended.

"It should be soon," we said, actually believing it.

Mother took her to Lay St. Christophe. When mother returned, she said the place was nice, with all the proper facilities to help people in grandmother's predicament. It was out in the country and operated by nuns. It had beautiful gardens, with chapel mass held every day. Grandmother would be happier there than with us. She'd have good care. I didn't have the heart to go see her during that winter, though mother went often.

The war, seemingly at a stalemate, showed no sign of ending and father wasn't able to go on leave and visit us. All seemed at a standstill. Rationing became more severe with coal harder to get; we were cold. We were thankful that Grandmother Braux wasn't with us; she would've been so cold in her room. There was little milk, too, needed for the foods she could eat. In February, grandmother's condition worsened.

The priest told us she couldn't live much longer. Mother went to stay with her at Lay St. Christophe for a while.

One day, mother came home and told me grandmother had died—very peacefully, as if going to sleep, and only asking for my father who she thought was by her side. Mother didn't contradict her. I'm sure father, in his mind, felt he was at her side.

My grandmother was gone.

We sent father a telegram. He received a 48-hour leave for the funeral. His captain, a priest, came with him. It was the nicest gesture. But father needed to return quickly to the Maginot Line. This, I believe, was one of the saddest of the many sad days in our lives during these times.

Father felt extremely pessimistic about the coming battles. He told us we'd certainly be occupied by Germany, and very shortly. The French soldiers didn't have a chance, trapped in the Maginot Line. They probably wouldn't get out alive, or if they did, the Germans were sure to capture them.

Would they fight? Yes, he said, if properly supplied with ammunition. Presently, however, he had a gun but no shells. What could he and most of the troops do? He was despondent and we all feared for the future. He prepared us for the eventuality of invasion and occupation. He was terribly worried about us, and we for him. When saying our farewells, we felt numb.

Five years would pass before we saw him again—he was 38 years old in 1940 but when returning, he'd look 60. Though never having met a German, I felt a dull hatred building up inside. My childhood definitely was gone.

Mother and I were two lost souls, only able to move on by focusing on daily activities. She left for work at 7 o'clock in the morning and returned at 7 p.m. I attended school from 8 to 5 o'clock, and then had church activities. I also entered the conservatory of music, with classes on Wednesday evenings and Saturday mornings. I visited with friends for a short time in the evenings. On Sundays, we'd get together with the family, but with very little laughter. The war and waiting for whatever fate loomed ahead were the topics of conversation. No joy for us.

We kept going, very much in the dark about the military situation. We didn't trust whatever news we heard. Conflicting reports said the Germans were coming, but then, no they weren't. The French army was resisting and pushing back the Germans, but other accounts said our troops were retreating, escaping to the south, and all was lost. We didn't know what to believe anymore, so we didn't believe anything and simply remained scared.

Sometime in April, Aunt Suzanne was badly injured in a roadway accident when she and Uncle Émile were driving to Lunneville to deliver vegetables to restaurants. As they approached the city in a small truck, a tire blew out. Thinking the loud sound was an exploding bomb, Aunt Suzanne jumped out of the truck and fell to the road under the car. Unable to stop fast enough, Émile drove over her leg, crushing it at the knee. She was hospitalized in terrible pain for several weeks with a cast up to her thigh.

Hitler's long anticipated main attack finally came in May 1940—a trying time for everyone. Soon, the Germans were approaching Nancy from the northwest and the south. Rumors were they'd be here any day. We waited in anguish as the French army crumbled, as did British and French forces in Belgium.

At the hospital, anyone not in critical condition, including Aunt Suzanne, was sent home. Uncle Émile and their daughter, Paulette, took care of her the best they could.

People by the thousands now attempted to leave Nancy, heading south—some intending to go to relatives or friends, while others hoped to find someone, anywhere, who'd take them in. Mother decided we should give it a try. We packed a large suitcase as full as we could, and filled up bags to carry.

My cousin, Auguste Ququ, came to carry the suitcase to the railway station for us. He could hardly pick it up. After many grunts and jokes, we reached the Gare St. Jean. We found ourselves amidst thousands of frantic people, all being told train service was postponed for an indefinite time. We waited hopefully, but finally gave up, rationalizing that staying home probably was safer anyway. And it was—later we heard of the tragedies occurring to this exodus of people, due to wartime hazards when out on the roads, as well as for leaving their homes empty and susceptible to plundering or German requisition.

The next day, we visited Aunt Suzanne at her residence in Essey, adjacent to northeast Nancy. She wasn't doing well and begged mother and me to stay and help. She needed so much physical care and was terrified about the arrival of the Germans. We returned home, packed a few things, closed our apartment, and went to stay with the Huguins. It wasn't pleasant; even when bed-ridden and in pain, Aunt Suzanne remained the tough taskmaster I'd known in the past. She turned mother and me into maids in a few minutes. Food was scarce, which was a special problem in the Huguin household as they'd always been enormous eaters. Mother and I almost wished the Germans would arrive and get things settled, so we could get out of this situation and return home.

An awful additional shock came on June 10 when Italy declared war on France. We knew of Mussolini's fascist views but couldn't understand this treacherous act. Now, both German and Italian planes attacked trains and roadways full of refugees. So many were killed; it was appalling.

On a Sunday morning, someone in the Huguins' neighborhood told us the Germans were at St. Avold, just a few kilometers away. A small contingent of French troops set up positions in a garden at a corner of the street. At noon, a lieutenant came to get some lettuce for their lunchtime salad. He said the Germans would be here that evening or the next day, depending on how much resistance the French troops could give. We were astounded! No matter how much we understood the inevitability of this coming event, we'd always hoped for a miracle.

I went to Marcelle Bérin's home beyond the Huguins' garden. Her daughter Suzanne had long been my friend. I told them what the lieutenant said. But all was quiet at the moment, just like on any other summer day. Marcelle asked me to wait a few minutes; she wanted to pick some roses from her garden to give to my ailing Aunt Suzanne. While she did this, my friend Suzanne and I roamed in the garden. Mr. Bérin, who wouldn't survive the occupation, a fine man, gave me a dark red rose (which I still have).

We heard some noises in the direction of the French soldiers— an explosion, then several more! A few minutes later, objects began

"Mother in Aunt Suzanne's garden after the war, the summer of 1947. The water tower behind her was rebuilt after being knocked down in the fighting."

whistling around us. I took the roses from Mrs. Bérin and ran to the garden by Aunt Suzanne's house. As I passed a water reservoir, I felt the wind from these whistling objects all around me, heard them striking the water tank, and got squirted by water spouting from the holes.

When I got to the bottom of the garden, Cousin Michel was coming for me. He grabbed me, practically carrying me off my feet, and made a dash for the inner courtyard. Mother was waiting for me, held by Cousin Paulette, who wouldn't let her go any further. Everyone cried out in absolute panic. Actually, I was kind of proud of myself for running through the machine gun bullets. I'd passed right between the French and German positions as they were fighting. A few days later, we found hundreds of shell casings in the garden.

Aunt Suzanne remained in bed, in mental and physical agony. She wanted us to hide in the basement, leaving her alone. We couldn't move her, nor leave her. Mother laid beside her while Uncle Émile, my cousins Michel and Paulette, and I crouched against the wall below the windows.

Bullets hit the house here and there, mainly upstairs above us, and then picked up in intensity. Then the French stopped firing. The Germans approached a short while later. We couldn't see them yet, but knew they were about a block away from the rumble of tanks and other vehicles. We peeked above the window sill, seeing several tanks and strange, clumsy-looking trucks mounted with high-powered weapons. Soldiers advanced alongside holding infantry weapons. Some also carried strange objects looking like a can with a handle; soldiers had them sticking out of their boot tops, too. These were grenades, we later learned. Our imaginations hadn't been exaggerating; the Germans looked as evil, if not more so, than we'd expected! If designed by the devil, he'd surpassed himself.

The small unit of French soldiers had resisted until their last bullet, then walked out with their hands up, and crying. I'd seen two Germans fall when hit, and several others sat on the street holding their hands over wounds. The tanks and trucks kept advancing, but some Germans stopped to seize the French prisoners. Several French soldiers bled, with some held up by their comrades. The lieutenant who'd come for lettuce was brought out dead, in a wheelbarrow dripping his blood. Our hearts sank further.

My aunt and mother couldn't see, so we whispered to them, telling them what was happening. Many Germans were coming, walking close to the houses on either side of the street, carrying rifles and machine guns, and some with a grenade in one hand and revolver in the other. To our surprise, hundreds also came along on bicycles, with weapons slung under their arms. I believe they couldn't see our faces, blocked by the busily-patterned crochet curtains that Aunt Suzanne had put up so passersby couldn't see inside.

One thing worried us. As they carefully looked around, practically every one of them at one time or another stared intently in the direction of the Huguins' upstairs windows. Why was that? It frightened us! For several hours, German troops passed by. I can't presume to give a number. Uncle Émile sat on the floor, sobbing. I went to mother's arms. We knew how defeated we were, with no remnant of hope left in our hearts. We listened to the tramping of their boots. For those of us who heard this during the German victory, we'll always recall it in our minds. Pain beyond words—I feel it still and always will.

Grandmother Faucheur's stories of past wars contained not a word of exaggeration when she explained her feelings. I felt every one of them, too, and more. Around 6 o'clock that evening, we opened the door a crack. All seemed peaceful. The Germans had set up machine guns at the corners of the street, but only stood around as if they didn't see us. Almost everyone went out their front door for a few seconds, getting a quick look.

Shortly, we heard the *Garde Champêtre* drum announcement, calling people to come out. We timidly stepped outside. A sort of procession was coming along the main thoroughfare. Here came the mayor—ceremonially dressed in top hat, with *cocarde* and all—the priest, and city officials, one carrying a white flag. German officers met them, the mayor handed a French flag to a German, and a few words were exchanged.

It was official. We were under German occupation. We still heard fighting off in the distance. After seeing the mass and power of German arms, we didn't hope they could be pushed back. Our distress was complete.

Since we were by the door, we looked up at the window that claimed the Germans' interest. We laughed in our misery. It was the window to the junk room above the garage, something of an attic. An old, blackish, metal pipe stood in the window; from the street it looked like a gun barrel.

We didn't know what to expect—whether the Germans would enter our homes or not, or search us. When the French lieutenant had visited us at noon, he advised Uncle Émile to hide his wall-mounted gun and World War I souvenirs, including a frame containing war medals and a pair of German boots, which were Émile's pride and joy. In his haste to find a hiding place for these things, Uncle Émile went to the garden, thinking to dig a hole and bury them. But time was too short—he simply went up the ladder to the top of the water tank and threw them in. He felt they'd be safe, even if some of the objects would be water damaged.

The irony of it all is that no German entered the house, but many were positioned in the gardens. They set-up a small cannon, and, of course, picked many of the Huguins' vegetables. The water tank was knocked down in the fighting, the contents spilled, and the boots, gun, and medals lay spread in the garden. Uncle Émile became mortified, but nothing happened to him. Whether the Germans saw those objects or not, we never knew.

That day ended, and several others went by. We had survived! We were breathing, eating what we could, and slept a bit, but the Germans were here. We heard and could see them. And even if we closed our eyes, we could smell their presence—no exaggeration! They had a peculiar sort of musty, sour scent, whether from their uniforms or food rations, we never knew. If we were near them, we could smell them. Their voices hurt our ears and the trod of their boots made us cringe. We were terribly unhappy with their presence.

Occupation

The first thing the Germans did was put up their flags, the *croix gammée*, the swastika. It hurt. It hurt so badly. Then they marched. They marched to their loud—and to our ears, barbaric—music. We felt transported back to the Middle Ages.

Within a week, all the shelves in the stores were nearly empty. The Germans sneered at us for our love of pastries and champagne, but it was incredible with what speed they purchased the things they couldn't get in Germany. They bought up practically everything in sight with occupation money—in other words, basically worthless money. They bought up toothpaste, brushes, and soap. They acted like children in a toy shop. We were astounded. They purchased lettuce and devoured it in the street. They bought sugar, eating the cubes right out of the box. Were they so hungry? Some felt sorry for them, until realizing they were a horde of locusts, starving us.

The next thing on the agenda was the regulations, increasing as
the weeks went by. *Verboten* was their favorite word—"Forbidden!" A
French person might've not cared to do some certain thing, but if told
it now was forbidden, he or she couldn't help but feel they "must" do it.
The Germans discovered this the hard way. In their obedient country
they hadn't learned of the many ways around *verboten* that the French
quickly worked out. Curfews were an example. If they'd shot on sight
all the French people in the streets during curfew (all with perfectly
prepared excuses for being out at night!), the Germans would've lost the
war in a few days using up all their ammunition.

Mother helped Grandmother Faucheur in her vegetable business
to add to our income. To do so, she'd go to the wholesaler to queue at
5 a.m., two hours before the overnight curfew was lifted at 7 a.m. She'd
carry some lettuce in her bicycle basket to explain her purpose for being
out. If she gave lettuce to a German patrol, they smiled at her and let
her go. After the first time, she took as many heads of lettuce as could
fit into her basket and never had trouble going out in the early morning
darkness.

Everyone had a good reason for breaking curfew. For example, it was
amazing the number of doctors and nurses who needed to save gravely
ill people in the middle of the night. It went along these lines for a while,
until the Germans finally caught on and tightened the noose around our
neck. By then, quite a few people had managed to escape from France,
but not enough. I will later discuss the plight of so many.

Aunt Suzanne remained in bad health, with her leg not healing
properly. We remained with her several more weeks, even though it was
safe for us to go home. Suzanne very much needed mother's assistance.
She eventually recovered somewhat, though had difficulty in walking,
needing canes. To my relief, we finally returned to my friends and our
own home.

In the following weeks and months, a portion of the French soldiers
managed to return. Both Mr. Kronemaker and Mr. Guissiani, living on
the two levels below us, came back, having escaped from the Germans

Great Britain

Calais

Belgium

Lille

Germany

Luxem-
bourg

Coastal military zone
("Atlantic Wall")
entry prohibited

Metz

Lorraine

Paris

Nancy

Zone of
German
settlement—
Return of
refugees
prohibited

Strasbourg

Brest

Alsace

Switzerland

Occupied Zone
German military occupation
from November 1942:
Northern Zone

DEMARCATION LINE

Vichy

Free Zone
from November 1942:
Southern Zone

Italy

Bordeaux

*Italian
occupation
zones*

Nice

Marseille

Toulon

Spain

Occupied Zone

With the Franco-German armistice on June 22, 1940, the Nazis exacted full monetary costs of the occupation from the French government, including the billeting of 300,000 German soldiers. The occupiers imposed strict censorship, severely restricted travel, abrogated civil liberties, and established internment camps. French clocks were advanced 1 hour to German time. Ironically, the Germans themselves banned Hitler's own book, *Mein Kampf*, because French people might read it and learn of the Nazis' disparaging views of France.

Plundering of the French industrial and agricultural economy began, lasting throughout the occupation. One-half to three-quarters of many foodstuffs—grain, oils, dairy livestock, etc.—were sent to Germany, with only perishables such as fruits and vegetables generally being exempted. Vast amounts of manufactured goods and raw materials—coal, minerals, leather, etc.—also were expropriated for German military and civilian use.

During the occupation, the nation's Gross Domestic Product plummeted. With the Vichy government's assistance, the Nazis also sent 1,100,000 French citizens into forced and voluntary labor in Germany.

Relatively few private automobiles were seen on French streets—most owners put their vehicles into storage, while the Germans requisitioned other vehicles. Without petroleum imports and due to wartime restrictions, France experienced extreme gasoline shortages. Consequently, bicycle use increased exponentially among the French population.

Though people on the streets often appeared well dressed, sometimes even fashionably so, hunger pangs afflicted most, negatively affecting overall health particularly for urban dwellers, the young, and elderly. Dietary shortages frequently caused stunted growth among French youths.

In two years, Gestapo (Secret State Police), SS (*Schutzstaffel*: Protective Echelon), and other Nazi party constabulary, along with French collaborators such as the neo-fascist *Milice*, infiltrated society in search of dissidents and opponents. Eventually, 90,000 (26%) out of 350,000 Jews in France were sent to concentration camps. Many Jews hid in urban areas, or escaped detection in the vast French countryside and in the Vichy and Italian zones where anti-Semitic measures were less severe.

In 1940, 1,575,000 French prisoners of war were herded toward Germany. Eventually, 24,600 died, 71,000 escaped, 320,000 were paroled for disabilities and sickness, and 220,000 were released under various agreements with the Vichy government. In 1944, 940,000 POWs still remained in Germany, held as factory and farm workers, and as a bargaining chip to impose further concessions from Vichy.

by wearing civilian clothes. For us, however, many were the hours spent on the balcony waiting for father. There was no sign of him—no mail, no phone call, nothing! We feared the worst—either he'd been killed or was held captive. We prayed, we cursed, but mainly we hated. The hate of a woman losing a man is fierce. The hate of a daughter of 13 is immeasurable. My hate was fire, consuming me.

Our life returned to a somewhat normal pace when my schooling started again in October. We tried to ignore the German multitude around us, gave up hope for father's return, and went on with daily chores.

Mother and I were becoming like sisters as we learned to live together in these challenging times. I'd grown up fast recently, really no longer a child. Eventually, I'd watch over our financial affairs. Mother, only 17 years my elder and youngish looking, didn't seem much older than I. In time—when making similar dresses from the same roll of hard-to-get cloth—we often looked like sisters when dressing up and going out.

Some of our neighbors who'd left Nancy during the exodus drifted back—exhausted, often ill. Frequently, they'd lost so much. How glad we were, having stayed at home. Some people's homes were now occupied by the Germans, who requisitioned empty houses wherever they found them. Other returning residents found their furnishings stolen or vandalized. The tragedies and difficulties were too numerous to assess totally, though people helped each other as best they could and as their means allowed. The Germans also seized garages for their vehicles, plus government and business buildings for administering the iron hand of occupation.

A friend of mine from across the street—Jean, a schoolmate—was killed by a land mine when coming back toward home. The Germans had mined the roads in case French troops attempted to return. When I knew Jean, as befitting the unwritten rules between boys and girls, we hardly spoke to each other or were ever together. But I'd watch him from my balcony and wrote to him. He sent me poetry. We were children learning to love. I was "faithful" to another boy, Jacques Pinnel, but rejoiced in the poems Jean sent me. I never knew whether he composed the poetry himself or copied them from books.

After Jean's death, I couldn't bear looking at his twin brother, who came back unscathed. I hated the Germans! The hate grew and grew! I can still hear it—they killed Jean, they killed so and so, and they tried to kill our minds.

Within months, our views of the Nazis hardened ever more. How did most of us view the Germans? They were known for being clean—their country's streets and houses were notably clean. They'd also cleansed whatever they found in their path if it didn't say "Heil Hitler." Yes, they were clean. Nazis killed and cleansed. France was soon to be cleansed. Regulations and the Gestapo saw to it.

The French were to be cleansed, inside and out. Hardly any food first of all; they took our food so our bowels would be clean. They took away our radios so our ears would be clean. They felt if we listened to BBC broadcasts from England, we'd certainly be very unclean. They would soon begin cleansing the country of Jews, Gypsies, and communists, as well as anyone they perceived as protesting against them.

German soldiers bought up most of the perfume and makeup in our stores. They claimed that the French were decadent in the use of such things. Why did they want these items? Strange for them to buy such decadent things! When the German army women came, the *souris grises* (grey mice), we wondered if under their unbecoming uniforms they wore French underwear that their men bought. These women certainly used our lipstick and perfume. I suppose that on them, such pure Aryans, it wasn't decadent!

Is hatred showing? Yes, I began to hate, and I never stopped, because there was no redeeming factor against doing so.

Now that we were being purgated, we were told that some Frenchmen were helping the Germans in this mass cleaning—as if the Nazis couldn't do it alone! We thought we'd reached the depth of misery. No, apparently we hadn't because our World War I hero, Marshal Philippe Pétain, joined them, as well as our new puppet premier, Pierre Laval. They sold the last of our pride. The Vichy government was our moral end. I was too young to fully know what this all meant, but the pain on the adults' faces was contagious. It didn't take long for the youngsters to catch on. We hated fiercely. It consumed us.

School began on time in October, as if all was normal despite the German presence. I'd finished my schooling for the *certificat d'études*, *premièr ordre*, a second examination and only needed to take the test, which had been cancelled in June because of recent events. I'd taken the exam and passed. What next? The secondary *lycée* wasn't organized, so I needed to wait.

In the meantime, I simply stayed in school, doing the same work all over again, and with the same master teacher, Madame Étienne, almost as great a tragedy for me as the German occupation. They hadn't touched me, but she had; the physical punishments in her class were legendary—what to do?

The Vichy Government

The new *État Français*, a right-wing, authoritarian, reactionary government—anti-parliamentarian, anti-secular, and anti-Semitic—was led by the collaborationist, Pierre Laval, and the WWI hero of the Verdun battle, Marshal Philippe Pétain. Vichy detested the 1789 revolution's democratic principles long adopted by France in the slogan, "Liberty, Equality, Fraternity," and replaced it with "Work, Family, Fatherland."

After the Nazi victory in 1940, the Germans occupied the northern three-fifths of France while allowing the newly constituted French government based in the town of Vichy to control a "Free Zone" in the southern two-fifths of the country. The Vichy government maintained a small independent army and cooperated closely with German authorities, as well as the Italians occupying portions of southeastern France.

Vichy itself primarily coined the use of the term "collaboration." Those French people who willfully, or were forced, to collaborate with the Nazis came from all walks of life—businessmen, workingmen, farmers, police, clergy, intellectuals, etc. In addition to its jurisdiction of the "Free Zone," Vichy's authority extended to the Axis occupied zones when it didn't conflict with German and Italian administration.

This played into Hitler's design, as the arrangement with Vichy ended French military opposition and kept the powerful French Navy on the southern coast from British confiscation. Vichy also administered the overseas French empire, particularly North Africa. With Western Europe secure, except for Great Britain, the Nazi leaders launched their ultimate wartime goal on June 22, 1941—the destruction of the USSR and enslaving and starving Slavic populations in unbelievable reductions, gaining *lebensraum* (living space) for German colonists for an eventual vast "Greater Germany."

Vichy disdained Général de Gaulle and the Free French forces in England and Africa. Following the Allied assault on French North Africa in November 1942, the Germans and Italians occupied the Vichy sector, leaving the *État Français* severely weakened. Nevertheless, Vichy strived for full partnership in a "New Order" on the continent following a final Axis victory. Documentary evidence indicates, however, that Hitler never intended France to be anything but a weak, subservient, and exploited nation in the "New Europe."

Mother didn't want to make major decisions about my future education without father's approval. Two of my cousins, Paulette and Gilberte, and my friend Suzanne Bérin were enrolled in a Catholic school, also awaiting the end of the war before making a decision. This was the answer for now; I'd also attend the Sacré Coeur school. We chose our courses. I took sewing, geography, French, and history.

The public schools were ordered to teach German; of course, we didn't learn much of it. Our teacher, Madame Étienne, to her credit, had told us the first day that she didn't plan to teach it, only meeting the requirements in minimal form. We purchased the book and notebook, never opened them, learned to count to 10 in German, and then forgot about the matter. The Sacré Coeur school I now began attending wouldn't even pretend; they didn't even mention the teaching of German.

I was very happy in that school. The rigid discipline, however, soon curtailed my playful and talkative ways. I erred once and was told that the Mother Superior wanted to see me in her office. I was sure I'd get the ruler as so often happened in public school. No; she was stern but gentle, only asking whether I regretted my bad conduct. I said I did. She said no matter, I must think carefully about my behavior, which was a matter between God and me—He knew about all my actions, good or bad. She told me to go in peace and love.

I was astounded. So, life could be that way. One was responsible only to oneself in front of God. I'd been told so in church, but hadn't adopted it in daily life—only to large decisions, not everyday small occurrences. I needed to review my own actions and how it affected the people around me.

Other questions came up when talking with Mother Superior. Why were the sisters such happy people? Because Jesus told them to be happy. What was Jesus in their life? They were married to him—married to him as my mother to my father. They wore a wedding ring as my mother did.

Pain and misery afflicted people all around me; what could I do to help as Jesus asked? I said my greatest wish was to become a nun and assist people. Mother Superior said she needed to speak to my parents, because until age 21, I couldn't make this decision for myself. Furthermore, even if my parents agreed, I needed several years of studies as a novice. To all this I agreed. She said if I proceeded through the whole program, surely the war would be over by then, and perhaps I could work in Africa where teachers always were most needed. In my enthusiasm I was ready to do anything, simply to do my share to eradicate all this evil surrounding us. If Jesus was willing to marry me, I was ready.

Mother came to Mother Superior for an interview, but lo, both said I must wait; I was too young. Later they talked again, but again mother said she couldn't make a decision until father's return. What if he was dead? Couldn't she make the decision by herself? I grew despondent and knew then that anything regarding my future depended on me alone. It was certainly a burden for a 13-year-old girl. I dropped the plan of becoming a nun, but not the idea of doing something. Something! What? I was like a volcano about to erupt.

As time went by, several young men a few years older than me, including my Cousin Roger, simply decided to disappear. In order to protect their families from the German police, we didn't even mention their going. We just knew they'd gone south. In time, words like *Résistance*, *France Libre*, and comments about "the underground" were heard. "Shh! Don't talk about it. The Germans will get us!" What did people mean? All we knew was that some men began leaving, disappearing from their homes within minutes, sometimes with meals left on the table—where were they? "Shh!—don't talk about it!" Everywhere we felt as though someone could be listening. We looked over our shoulders, beginning to distrust everyone.

As a child, I'd learned to read and write through the goodness of the two nuns who gave me a love of history and living—a disciplined and restricted living, perhaps, but with love for others. Today I believe that much of everything I became was derived from them. I hope a fraction of this has remained with me. For the present, I kept attending the Sacré Coeur school. I cleaned up my tongue. One time when confessing I'd used coarse language, a priest asked what I gained from it. I couldn't say. As penance he told me not to eat chocolate for a week. Did he notice I was quite plump? At any rate, I've never used that kind of language since.

I studied diligently, and also attended the music conservatory, under a delightful teacher, Mr. Roux. Not being musically gifted, I didn't do very well, but kept on attending. I loved that building. From our study room, we could hear the taps from the ballet room. Orchestra practices as well as opera rehearsals for the municipal theater also were heard. In the hall and stairs we'd meet the big name singers from Paris and all over. In addition, I made good friends, such as Nadine, who had danced in the ballet troupe since the age of 8. I forgot about everything else as she talked me into trying out for the ballet. Madame Comte, the ballet mistress, looked at me for half a minute, then said no; my body wasn't built for ballet, forget it. I was crushed.

I couldn't marry Jesus, I couldn't dance, and I couldn't fight the Germans. I was so helpless! "I couldn't" now became a litany in my mind.

Other good friends in music class, Suzanne and Pierre, helped me a great deal in overcoming my malaise. Pierre suggested that if I tried and practiced hard, I could learn a musical instrument. All the students went to La Lorraine, a *brasserie* in the center of town where a fantastic orchestra played for the diners. I went there with mother. Yes, the orchestra leader was fabulous. He taught violin at the conservatory and he told me I could sign up for his instruction. I could take private lessons to catch up with the regular class. I could go to his home a few blocks from mine. All could be the best of all worlds.

Mother, though, wasn't convinced. Again, father wasn't there to approve. She wouldn't buy a violin. Where could I find a violin? Where could I get the money to purchase one and pay for lessons? I couldn't be stopped. I explained my plight to Aunt Suzanne, who said she'd loan the money if I'd work in her garden. Yes, anything! I would've ploughed the whole earth!

In a week I had a violin, but no case, so I carried it in a bag. I went to my lessons, dancing all the way. Mother didn't know about it. I hid the violin under the bed and practiced while she was at work. Our neighbors swore to secrecy as long as I didn't practice when their babies were asleep.

I did odd jobs to pay for lessons, and walked everywhere to save my tram money. Mother became angry at her sister Suzanne for having me work so hard in the garden—for nothing, mother thought. But I was rather personally happy that year, with friends at home, church, school, and the conservatory. If I couldn't have all I wanted, at least I had part of it.

Mother remained extremely busy helping grandmother with the produce business, working afternoons at Frank's fur shop, and at night for her private customers. She was too tired to notice all my activities. I helped her in finishing some of the fur tailoring. She was unhappy about all the time I spent reading, so I learned to knit and read at the same time. I'm so thankful about this; it's something I still do today.

But the Germans remained, and still no news of father. We felt so much pain. We worked until we dropped off to sleep—to forget, I suppose. Mother became extremely thin and often had fainting spells. Insufficient food and our misery were the cause, the doctor said. I remained somewhat plump, but afflicted with bronchitis and anemia. All was not well!

We visited the family and went to the theater as before. I got in free, being a conservatory student, which was nice. I loved everything about the theater. I read plays and learned parts for myself. It became a love.

Father Is Alive!

After almost a year of occupation, a letter finally came from father—an open form-type letter. It said little—he loved us, was in a camp, loved us, was as well as could be expected under the circumstances, loved us, couldn't say more about his whereabouts, loved us, hoped we were well, loved us.

We were in heaven! He was alive! Now if we could just get rid of the Germans, life would be wonderful. However, England was doing badly, no one heard anything from America, and it looked like Russia was going down soon, just like France had. No hope anywhere!

The worst winter in decades had left us cold, hungry, and with little hope for the future. More people disappeared every day. The Germans' coupon system severely restricted the necessities—gas was so rationed that we could barely fry an egg (we got only one egg per person a month, often too old to be consumed). Sawdust was added to the slim piece of bread we received after waiting hours for it. The black market was rampant. Typhus killed many. We were now a country of women and old men. Every day was filled with tragedy.

But father was alive; how thankful we were about that!

We managed to take a bit of pleasure whenever possible by going to *brasseries*, concerts, movies, and the theater. While waiting in line for theater tickets, I overheard a conversation that changed my life in a great way. Two ladies ahead of me were discussing some person—a marvelous, talented person, a tremendous actor. I didn't pay all that much attention until they mentioned that this man's best friend was Pierre Richard-Willm. I listened carefully; Pierre Richard-Willm was my favorite movie actor. Like many youngsters, I was a great fan of movie stars, but he definitely was my "hero."

I couldn't resist. I asked those ladies who the person was they were talking about—this great friend of Pierre Richard-Willm. What, I didn't know him! Mr. Louis Fleurant, of course, who taught diction and drama at the conservatory. It was about 11 a.m. I bought our tickets, went to the conservatory, got Mr. Fleurant's address, and then walked over to his house that afternoon. I skipped school and all—something pushed me along like a hurricane.

To my sorrow, a very nice lady said he wasn't home, but asked if I'd come for a lesson. I lied, saying yes. She asked me to wait in a small office with a desk and chairs in front and behind. Photos hung on the walls—sure enough, including several of Pierre Richard-Willm.

After more than an hour of uneasy waiting, the door finally opened and a somber, distinguished looking gentleman walked in. He looked old to me, about 60—to me that was quite elderly. He asked: What was I doing here? I told him I wanted to take lessons. He said he didn't know me, that I was too young, had to be 16 to enter his classes, etc., so I needed to get out. I'd have to wait three years before I could apply to enter his conservatory classes.

I couldn't move from my seat. I begged, I cried, I simply had to get into one of his classes. He said the best he could do was to give me private lessons. Sure, I'd do anything. He quoted a fee of 30 francs per hour. Yes, I would pay that. He gave me an appointment for one lesson each week. Heaven—I'd discovered it! That's where God lived, and Mr. Fleurant seemed exactly like what God was supposed to look like.

Now I had to find the ways and means for my weekly sessions in diction and drama heaven. I already had the books he told me to get, or I could find them at the library. One hurdle crossed.

Second, how could I go every Thursday afternoon at 4 p.m. to Rue du Montet across town when I was supposed to be in school? I worked that out—I lied—telling the home economics teacher that I needed to go home and help mother.

Third—the money, 30 francs a week; 120 francs a month! Not impossible! Mother couldn't understand my newly acquired love for weeding Aunt Suzanne's garden. I'd get the money.

But no garden work is done in autumn and winter when I still owed Mr. Fleurant his fees. Finally, I told him the truth. He wondered why I hadn't revealed this to my mother? I said I feared she'd forbid me from taking lessons. He said he'd talk to her, adding that I should continue, that I was good, would be good when older, and he didn't want me to stop. I also said I had the same difficulties with my violin lessons. He was surprised, but said he'd help if he could.

Mr. Fleurant invited mother to tea on the pretense that his wife needed a fur coat repaired. Mother became suspicious when I wanted to go along, and more so when I seemed to know everyone there, including Madame Fleurant and her mother.

Mr. Fleurant spoke to my mother. Then his wife asked mother if she'd be willing to do fur handwork in exchange for my lessons. Poor mother was so shocked. How could I have managed all this for months without her knowledge? She was hurt and wanted me to end this right away. But she didn't know about Mr. Fleurant's powers of persuasion. His Molière, Racine, and Corneille's parts were never better than the performance he put on for mother. After a short time, we had coffee and cookies. Mother went home carrying Madame Fleurant's coat for repairs.

From then on, I told mother about everything I did, or wanted to do. She agreed that I was growing up. She wouldn't try to keep me as a "little girl" until father's return.

I only attended school half time, because I needed the spare hours to practice violin and learn my diction and drama lessons for Mr. Fleurant. I became so terribly anxious when going to his lessons. He was a most grueling teacher. I shook with panic before entering his house, and often left crying after he admonished me mercilessly. But I always came back for more.

One time when arriving for my lesson and ringing the bell, someone new opened the door. I almost fainted on the spot. Pierre Richard-Willm stood there, asking me to come in—Mr. Fleurant was a little late, but I could wait. I went to sit in the office—shaking, not believing what'd just happened. Mr. Fleurant soon came in with an amused smile, saying "Nice surprise for you!" He knew about my adoration for the famous actor. Needless to say, I wasn't very attentive in my lesson that day. How could I, knowing that He was in the house somewhere.

One day in early spring, Mr. Fleurant said, "It's time to prepare you for the entrance exam." What, did this mean I didn't have to wait for years? No, he'd try to get me into the conservatory, but I needed to take the exam like everyone else. No pull there. Several hundred students of all ages would be screened by a panel composed of director Catrien of the national theater, an actor from the *Comédie Française* in Paris, a professor from the *faculte des lettres*, a government representative for the arts, and several other people I didn't know—about 10 altogether. We were given a partner for reading an unprepared scene, answered questions, and walked and move around while taking whatever part we were told to. It sounded monstrous, and it was. Mr. Fleurant told me I could only be an auditor the first year, but that I was not to fail him. How could I fail him? One cannot fail God, can one?

I prepared, I cried, I cursed. If he didn't kill me first, I'd soon kill Mr. Fleurant! I took the exam. Thirty-two people were accepted and my name was on the list. Impossible to believe! For the first time my name appeared in the newspaper. For sure I was on my way.

Yes, on my way to something like the Gestapo training ground! We were told many tales about the Gestapo—this must've been something like it, but I'd found my niche. I loved everything and everyone there. The world of Racine, Molière, Corneille, all dissected, analyzed, taken apart, and put back together again with a real master—a master with a whip, but glowing with talent as he sat on the radiator. Of these good times, which were for me like a make-believe island in the storm of torment surrounding us, I will return later. I must relate the myriad of incidents which occurred in our lives outside of my personal paradise.

We worried about father as the months passed, but were learning to live without his presence. Many people had no news of their fathers, husbands, brothers, friends. We listened to the BBC every evening that we could. Mrs. Guissiani had a radio; we never asked how she acquired it (we'd stopped asking such questions). Madeleine Kronemaker and my mother went to the Guissiani's apartment as a matter of course to secretly listen to the BBC broadcasts, while I'd visit with Mrs. Guissiani's son, Pierrot.

Général Charles de Gaulle had made an historic speech on the BBC, urging us to persevere, that many men had joined him in forming the Free France movement. So many of us hoped that their loved ones and friends, from whom they hadn't heard news, were among the Free French forces in North Africa or England.

Pierrot Guissiani kept saying how much he wanted to get away and do something for France, but his mother needed him here. Finally, one day, he was gone. His parents said he left to visit his relative, Mr. Cadario, now in southern France. Mr. Cadario had a bad reputation as a collaborator for doing construction and architectural work for the Germans and supposedly getting rich in the process. I felt bad about Pierrot. Did he join in this ignominy? I hoped not. I was proved right. The Germans shot Mr. Cadario as a traitor, which made us all so sad, but this confirmed his loyalty to France. Of Pierrot Guissiani, we had no word.

Somewhat later, the Gestapo came looking for Mr. Guissiani, supposedly for counterfeiting food coupons. Pierre Guissiani turned himself in, knowing he was taking his son "Pierrot's" place, who indeed had been dealing in illegal coupons. The father and son had the same name, thus the "Pierre Guissiani" written on the coupons could be attributed to Mr. Guissiani. He spent six months in prison under the harshest treatment—beatings, starvation, and all the other pain the Gestapo knew how to inflict. But his son was free.

During this time, Mrs. Guissiani had a baby, Gerard. We assisted the best we could. Mrs. Kronemaker helped with the housework while I took care of the other Guissiani children, Micheline and Jeannot. Mother provided vegetables and whatever she could find on the black

"A view of the Blvd. Foch home after the war, with my daughter and son standing in front. The Guissianis lived on the 1st floor, the Kronemakers on the 2nd, and we occupied the top story. Mr. Zint resided on the 1st floor of the house at left, and collaborators owned the large building to the right."

market. Mrs. Guissiani was helpless with her husband in Gestapo hands; we all had to pitch in for people like her.

Mrs. Kronemaker's husband, Fernand, wasn't of much help to us, being gone most of the time. He was a locomotive engineer and desperately needed by the Germans. When he came home with a big grin, however, we felt good knowing that somewhere during his travels he'd witnessed a successful sabotage. Mrs. Kronemaker remained frightened for her husband. She didn't know whether he was involved in sabotage, but with him being such a staunch communist, we all suspected he was. If not, he certainly enjoyed seeing it occur.

Mother always kept in touch with her former employers, the Grundfelts. One day she arrived home in tears. I had trouble getting her to tell me what was wrong—she was so shocked! She didn't find the Grundfelts at home, even though they seldom went out due to their poor health and usually sent their daughter to do the shopping. Mother inquired at some neighbors, who told her the Germans took them away because they were Jews.

This was our first knowledge of the Jewish removal. Previously, they had to wear a yellow star, which made most of us protective of Jews—letting them get ahead of us in line, and doing small favors for them whenever we could. The Grundfelts' plight frightened us. They were as French as any of us, and both very ill—she could hardly walk and he had tuberculosis.

Mother also worried about her present employer, Mr. Frank, who also was Jewish, but as French as any of us. He shrugged it off, saying he'd heard rumors, but there was no reason for the Germans to bother him. He wouldn't hide. But the worst happened. The Gestapo broke into his house and seized him, leaving his wife, who wasn't Jewish. She was devastated. Mother and Mr. Lucien, another employee, helped her keep the business going. But eventually Mr. Lucien went to another furrier, so my mother was alone with Madame Frank. They took in only a small amount of work. It was difficult for Madame Frank, who hadn't learned much about furrier work; she'd only taken care of bookkeeping and correspondence. She would've been destitute without some work coming in.

Another abduction of Jews likewise hit very close to me. One morning when arriving at my violin teacher's residence for a lesson, I saw a large Jewish star painted on the door. I asked the neighbors about this and they recounted the now familiar details—a couple of days earlier the Germans took him and his family during the night. I didn't even know he was Jewish. His coat must've covered the star on his shirt. I ran home crying in misery, put my violin under the bed, and never practiced again. I later sold it. My pain and anger were without bound. I hurt, I hated.

This man had only one kind of politics, if music can be called that—he played in the national orchestra, and taught at the conservatory and at home. He also was a leader of the marvelous band at the La Lorraine *brasserie*. They never returned. We'd lost hope in the Germans having any feelings of humanity.

Earlier at the La Lorraine, in fact, mother and I had witnessed an incident leaving us extremely pessimistic about the Germans. My music teacher was playing. The room was full, with no empty seats. Two German SS men walked in, seemingly looking for seats. About 20 feet from us, two young Germans soldiers sat at a table enjoying the music while drinking beer. We saw the SS men talking to them. We couldn't tell what was being said, but within a few moments, one SS man took out his pistol and shot the two soldiers. We walked out as fast and quietly as we could. There must've been more than a hundred people in the *brasserie*. We all were stunned, realizing that if they did that to their own countrymen, we had no hope for ourselves.

The family of my long-time friend and neighbor, Jacques Pinnel, also became victims. His Jewish mother, and her sister and the sister's husband, were taken away. Jacques and his father weren't home at the time, so they were spared. This occurred just two houses away from where we lived. He and his father continued living in the home.

Some people still tried to ignore these things, but we couldn't be told it was only our imagination. More and more houses stood empty or were occupied by Germans. People we knew disappeared without a trace—whole families. In the beginning it was mainly Jews, or political rebels labeled as "communists" since they didn't bow down to the Vichy government. At the time, of course, the communists were heroes to us after Germany attacked Russia in June 1941.

We'd had so little hope, and now even less, if that was possible. Even my sweet, gentle Uncle Émile, who could've hardly stated our particular political or religious preferences, spent three months in jail. Someone denounced him for listening to the BBC; knowing my uncle, he probably fell asleep during the broadcast. Like Mr. Guissiani, he was beaten for no reason. Formerly a large man, he came home starved to a skeleton, ill with ulcers, and lice infected—all in just three months! The whole family was distraught.

Still no word arrived about my disappeared cousin, Roger Ququ—we just hoped he'd been able to join the Free French or Allied forces. His brother Auguste, who felt he should stay with the family and who thought nothing could happen to him, was drafted into German labor. Aunt Hélène heard from Auguste a few times, so at least we knew he was alive. It pained us when finding out he was building bunkers on the Atlantic Coast. A redeeming factor, however, was that we knew him to be a slow worker; we felt sure if the Germans weren't watching, he certainly wouldn't hurry the job. Thus Aunt Hélène, whose husband Louis died shortly before the war, was alone with her daughter, Gilberte.

Priests, nuns, doctors, and nurses disappeared. With it often being nearly impossible to get medical help, many illnesses remained untreated. Insufficient food aggravated the situation—the lack of nutrients and vitamins took its toll. Babies starved or died, as did elderly people without the stamina to queue at the shops, and also those people who couldn't find work and were afraid to apply at employment offices, fearing they'd be sent into forced labor. People without the money or ability to participate in the black market suffered most.

The Black Market

A negative term, but a means of existence and a way to beat the system imposed by the Nazis. What did the black market mean to my family and our friends? Mother could acquire vegetables, getting them from grandmother and her contacts in the countryside. Mother could then trade vegetables for cheese from a grocer instead of exchanging money. If she got two cheeses from the grocer, she could exchange one for a piece of meat from a butcher. Grandmother also could get butter from her friends out on the farms. Once I gave a butter loaf to a shoe repairman as payment for leather used in resoling a pair of shoes.

We also heard about the black market conducted in a "big way," with some individuals becoming rich practically overnight. People in some of these lucrative "deals," perhaps pretending to be collaborators, obtained hard-to-get gasoline and tobacco from the Germans.

To me it was a way to resist, regaining part of what the Germans took from us. We gave the Germans the nickname *dorifores* (potato beetle), because of their speed and ability in cleaning us out of food.

The Germans worked hard to curb our ingenuity. We couldn't understand why they used so much manpower to harass ordinary people who tried to smuggle a few eggs or a pair of stockings. They did so for years, even when manpower shortages late in the war reduced them to drafting 14- and 16-year-old German boys to fill their ranks on the Russian front.

People were searched in the street, on trams, and on trains. Grandmother escaped detection by guards several times when smuggling butter, meat, and eggs during trips between Inveaux and Nancy. She wore long, shapeless, voluminous dresses, attaching whatever she could to a belt worn underneath. She feared that butter might melt or eggs break, giving her away. Grandmother had a close call when a zealous German frisked her quite actively while ignoring her outrage and protests. She was lucky; someone nearby created a disturbance that distracted the German. Disturbances were usually set up to save people in tight situations. The German forgot all about my grandmother. She had quite a load—butter, bacon, and some other meat—under her dress. She fed much of our family this way; thanks to her we managed to get extra protein.

To get on a train, one needed a pass, issued by the Gestapo only in case of an emergency. It's amazing how many sick relatives grandmother had in the farming communities outside of Nancy.

Younger women pretended to be in late pregnancy, carrying food in special containers under their garments, giving the appearance of nothing amiss. Everyone had a favorite story about daring escapes from the German police. In hearing some of their exaggerations, they seemed to be carrying 100 pounds of sugar in their hat!

But our fear of capture wasn't exaggerated. One time on a tram, I carried a bottle of olive oil (about four months of the allowed ration) in my purse under my arm. A German soldier pressed against me in the crowded space. I couldn't move and feared he might feel the bottle. I was fortunate, but many times we saw people being arrested on the sidewalks, in stores, aboard trams, and elsewhere. Sometimes the Germans only confiscated what the person was carrying. But other times, for no worse of an offense, people were taken away and never seen again. All was according to their whim. They weren't particularly responsive to pretty girls or sympathetic to the elderly or sick.

We learned to smuggle in order to survive. Our future was shrinking—with survival often measured only in days, or less. Our future meant mother and I looking at each other across the table and one of us saying, "Alright, it's my turn, I'll go see so and so, he may have something." We didn't know what; we didn't care—just as long as we had something to put in our mouths to chew.

We had some strange, lucky finds, amusing now when looking back. One time mother got a hold of six dozen oysters, but we had no refrigerator—since the Nazis took them away to Germany. Of course, we split our oysters with the neighbors, but have you tried eating three dozen oysters in one day?

Mother sometimes met with the owner of a fish market and traded vegetables for a live fish. We'd put the fish in a pail of water in the kitchen. One time, a large carp jumped out. I tried catching and putting it back in the water. This was extremely difficult because the fish was slippery and strong. Finally, I got it back in, but again it jumped out. I closed the kitchen door so it wouldn't flop into the dining room. Actually, I was afraid.

But not as afraid as I was of live chickens, which we acquired from time to time. One rooster was so scary, so powerful. We attached his foot to a line tied to the kitchen table, but the rooster pulled the table around. We were afraid that some neighbor might hear the commotion. Of course, everyone was used to hearing strange sounds, but no one asked any questions. When my poor mother had to kill and dress some of these creatures, I simply disappeared. I know now that she overcame fear and disgust to feed me. Like all good mothers, she was determined to provide for me, as her mother had done for her. I hope I thanked her enough.

In their sadistic manner, the Germans did their best to undermine us. For instance, we were allowed a few ounces of meat once a week, paid for with coupons, but the Germans knew that the majority of people were Catholic and obeyed the rule of only eating fish, and no meat, on Fridays. Consequently, the German authorities permitted butchers to only open on Fridays. The church quickly gave dispensation from this rule, but many people, including mother and I, still wouldn't eat meat on Friday. We'd cook it late, eating after midnight. No, we wouldn't let the occupiers get to us—we lost weight, but not our spirit.

The Germans considered it a great offence for people to deal in food and coupons on the black market. The cost was high for those getting caught. Indeed, the counterfeiting of coupons became a big business with high stakes, usually conducted by the underground. Mr. Guissiani spent those six months in jail because his son was on a list of suspects. If they'd found any proof, Mr. Guissiani would've been shot.

We needed to be extremely careful when trading on the black market as some people were Nazi sympathizers or were planted by the Gestapo to interdict this activity. Also, there were some people needing favors from the Germans for one reason or another, and they'd turn people in. It was best to obtain genuine coupons from grocers or business people by making exchanges using other goods. Money often was of little use. A person might be rich, but would starve if unable to barter and trade coupons for things needed.

Grandmother spent less and less time in distributing produce, leaving it mostly to mother, who acquired quite a "know-how." Mother's shy, gentle personality served her well when bartering. Restaurants were desperate to obtain vegetables and fruits—they'd pay in the coupons that the customers used for their meals. Mother exchanged some of the coupons with farmers, and so on—it was amazing how many times the same coupons got around. It was a game.

Mr. Piquemale, our Spanish friend when we formerly lived on Rue du Général Duroc, was of great help to us. He managed the largest import produce wholesaler in the region, La Maison Oliver, specializing in citrus fruit grown in Spain. The other large wholesale house in Nancy was Maison Monot. Regardless of our friendship with Mr. Piquemale, mother always waited patiently in line with the others at Oliver. Mr. Piquemale provided mother with some of the best and most generous amounts. How thankful we were to him.

We'd put in an order for produce for the following day, but couldn't choose the amount or type. We took whatever came our way. My job was to notify our individual customers, grocers, and restaurant owners when it was available. They'd come to pick it up at our storage space, a rented basement in a very old house on Rue Notre Dame, located only about a block from the wholesale firm. The cool and damp basement proved ideal for keeping fruits and vegetables fresh.

One day mother struck great fortune. Mr. Piquemale got her a load of carrots, which at the time were like gold. It was a load full to the top! She was astounded, seeing riches in front of her eyes. But we only had a few hours to transport the carrots from the railroad car to our storage place, five or more blocks away. I rounded up most of the family and all the friends I could find, while mother found an elderly man with a hand cart. We got busy—working hard to get it done. When people saw us unloading carrots at our storage room, we began fearing that someone might break in if we weren't around. That night, mother, Aunt Hélène, and I stayed in that damp, smelly (mainly of carrots) basement. We were frightened; it was kind of horrible.

But the next day, all the carrots were sold. What a boon. Mr. René, a grocer, told us that a woman customer cried with joy when told she could take all she wanted. We made so many people happy, which greatly pleased us for having made the effort. Of course, it also was a good business deal. That's how I acquired the bottle of olive oil that I carried in my purse on the tram.

I'll always remember our incredulity when standing in front of that load of carrots. But it was almost topped by pumpkins on another occasion, for me anyway. In late fall 1941, mother was ill and unable to go to the wholesalers, so I volunteered. I stood in line at Maison Monot—no one knew what might be available, if anything. When the doors opened and we went in, all we saw were pumpkins—large ones, about three feet in diameter. Most people left discouraged. Mother told me to get anything, no matter what—but pumpkins? And their size? I bid on one, but was told the minimum was for three. Ok—if I could take one I could take three. People laughed at me. Here I was with huge pumpkins, again with no transport. Our storage room was about two blocks away with streets to cross, but I made it. I rolled them, one after another. I still don't believe I made it. As least I gave some enjoyment to war weary passersby.

Again, it was a good deal. The grocers were happy, and we sold one to a restaurant. French people do not make pumpkin pie, but rather pumpkin soup. It was a treat. When coming home, I felt afraid to tell mother, but she was delighted—I'd done well. We never knew where such large pumpkins were grown. I've never seen such large ones again. I think it must've been the kind used for Cinderella's coach.

Another constant and difficult task was the hunt for fuel. We had only one stove to warm our apartment. During pre-war times, we burned a special kind of coal, but this ended when the Germans confiscated the good coal for themselves. Now, only coke was available, and in small quantities. The coke was the residue left after gas was extracted from coal at the electrical works. It was of marginal use to us even if we had a lot, because it burned poorly in our stove. We'd burn what we could, just to get a little warmth. Firewood burned up quickly, but we could use it. Not far away, trucks hauled the remains of a bombed-out house to a landfill. We youngsters, taking our bags and baskets, were the first to scavenge for pieces of wood among the debris. When word got around, a mass of people showed up. I carried home several bags of wood. What a boon!

Another time, we were allowed to take wood out of the *forêt de Haye*, about three miles up a steep hill, just north of Nancy. My friend Denise Bredin and I got a hold of a wheelbarrow and went into these muddy woods, where some boys cut the firewood. We put what we could on the old wooden wheelbarrow and started down the slope, with one of us in front keeping the load from rolling too fast, while the other struggled to keep the wheelbarrow going straight. It was horrendous—we cried all the way down, but made it home.

On another occasion, when walking with Denise near the Rue de Mon-Désert bridge over the railroad tracks in town, we noticed people filling sacks from a coal pile on the quay. I had a pass card for going in to collect vegetables, so we entered through a nearby gate. I was told that if we brought containers, we could buy coal. I left Denise to watch over what we purchased and made a dash to find the old man with a push cart who'd hauled the carrots for us. He kept on helping us now and then. He lived in a disreputable house on a very disreputable street, but I ignored fear and pride, and with bated breath went to find him. Fortunately, he was there. I also went a few blocks away to our storage place, gathered up some sacks, and off we went back to the railroad. Being gone for such a long time, I feared Denise might leave and the coal would be gone. It was dark and snow began falling.

But Denise was still there! We filled the sacks by hand, with the snow making the coal sticky. Coal dust covered Denise and I. We were so happy! We loaded up and took our fantastic treasure to the storage basement. We couldn't take it all the way home; our old helper wouldn't do it. We didn't blame him—he couldn't possibly make it. We gave him a bag of coal as payment; he thanked us with tears in his eyes. He lived with an old lady, a former prostitute, whom he loved very much. He was desperate—she was ill and shaking because their rooms were so cold.

One of my family's friends, who had a small truck, brought our two bags of coal to my house. By careful rationing, it kept us warm for several weeks. What a find during the horrible winter of 1941!

At night, the temperature in our rooms dropped below freezing. In the morning, the water pressure in our home was very low because of the electricity restrictions imposed during the occupation. To ensure having water in the morning for washing up, mother filled a basin, leaving it in the kitchen sink overnight. Lo, one morning when I went to use the basin, it was frozen solid. I could hardly believe it! I made a fire in the heating stove to melt the ice.

If I'd used the low flame of our gas stove, on the other hand, it would've taken all day. Gas was restricted to low amounts due to rationing. It was only on from 6 to 8 a.m., 11 a.m. to noon, and 5 to 7 p.m. At other times, we used an alcohol lamp, if we could find alcohol. For that, we needed to buy it on the black market, or know someone who somehow got it from the Germans.

Yes, it was a cold winter. So cold that even my grandmother felt sorry for the German soldiers. The officers wore magnificent uniforms, but the soldiers, often enough, were poorly dressed. If they were tall, their jackets and pants might hardly meet at midriff, exposing them to the cold. They filled their boots with straw and newspapers. Sometimes we saw Germans taking scarves and gloves from people in the streets.

How we feared for father! It was even colder in northern Germany where we deduced he was—around Dortmund. Though only a little more than 200 miles northeast, he might as well have been on the moon. We received a form-type letter from him about every six weeks, but he wasn't allowed to tell us his location. The letters were written in pencil only and sometimes a few words were blacked out or erased by German censors. Adolf Hitler's profile appeared on the postage.

Somehow we arrived at the conclusion, correct as it turned out, that he was in the general direction of Dortmund. I believe he mentioned something about a river that was stopped or some such thing. Looking on a map, we saw a dam in that area. Later, this caused us terrible concern when hearing that British bombers destroyed the dam, flooding the whole area and drowning many people. For weeks we worried about him.

Innuendoes in the letters provided some glimpse of his situation: "I thought I would never be a farmer, but life changes for some people." Or, "When you send a package include children's toys, so I can make friends of my neighbors." We concluded he was on a farm and on fairly good terms with the people, or else he wouldn't wish to give toys to children.

One thing worried us—he begged for Vaseline, used for frostbite. We couldn't find any for a long time, until finally getting it on the black market. But we could only send one package every six months via the Red Cross, so it took a long time for him to receive it. The packages also were limited to just two pounds—precious little could be sent this way. We found out when he came back that the Germans lied to the prisoners, telling them that the reason they received so few packages was because their families simply didn't send them. It was so cruel.

I knit him socks, caps, gloves. The socks he never received. Packages were always opened, so I suppose they were stolen. Maybe my knitting job on the gloves and hat was so poor that no German was tempted to take them. From the types of things that father asked us to send, we realized he had no idea of our situation. We felt helpless. He wanted coffee, sugar, chocolate, canned goods, underwear—many things.

Our coffee was brewed from grilled oats—oats put in a cake pan in the oven and roasted. Sugar couldn't be found; chocolate completely disappeared. We had no canned goods for the simple reason there was no metal to make cans; the canning factories were closed. We sent father some of his underwear that he had left at home, but he never received them. We were so distressed. Did he realize that we had to give up a month's ration of bread for one package of cigarettes?

In their pain, people began to lose control. Hate turned to rage. As some people expressed their feelings, they were taken away or shot.

Many became daring. Prostitutes killed their bed mates, and we praised them for it, or passed on their venereal diseases. Those who could joined the underground in little ways or larger ways, depending on their abilities.

The Underground

This was an illusive world, and appearances could be misleading. Pierrot Guissiani was labeled a "bad" son for leaving his family, supposedly to have fun. Being quite handsome, the gossip was he'd gone off with some girl. Even his parents thought so. I had to keep faith to survive; I was at the age when all was black and white. I hoped he'd joined the underground. I had to believe in some people—Pierrot was one.

One of our priests at nearby St. Thérèse was blamed for "seeing" one of his women parishioners, an unofficial scandal. In a less civilized society she would've been stoned to death. He disappeared. She was taken away by the Gestapo, never to be seen again. After the war we suspected both were involved in the *Résistance*.

We were terribly ashamed of a woman who lived on our own street. Her husband was a prisoner in Germany, yet she had a different German officer at her home practically every day, sometimes ranking as high as colonels. A beautiful woman, we half understood her for having some fun—these men came with flowers and champagne. We were heartbroken and our pride was hurt, until hearing she died of advanced syphilis shortly thereafter. We concluded she knew and did the damage to the Germans while she could. There was no penicillin to cure syphilis at that time. It wasn't pleasant, but many unsung heroes did what they could.

Many people who appeared to be collaborators actually were engaged in *Résistance* work. They often paid a high price in order to hide their involvement—mainly the loss of respect and love of family and friends. We despised some people for their apparent collaboration with the Germans—we thought they were traitors. Not until after the liberation did we learn about their actual patriotism. Did the Pétain government really help us to survive? That question will never be answered.

Sometimes the work wasn't heroic, but rather more humorous. We disliked a butcher in our neighborhood because he sold meat to

Germans, with a grin. We learned later he'd sprinkle the meat with some powder causing diarrhea. He did what he could without getting shot.

Our deepest despair came in 1942 and the first half of 1943, with England bombed, Russia losing, and America mostly silent except when invading North Africa, far away. When would they come to our rescue? Was it possible they wouldn't! Were we to starve and die? With our morale declining, could we stand up to it all? Some committed suicide in their despair.

Others had turned to collaboration for survival. To our sorrow, young men joined the *Milice*, a German-supported paramilitary police. By doing this, some avoided being sent to forced labor in Germany. Not every collaborator, however, was a good or frightened man or woman just trying to survive. Some people, including most of the fascist-like *Milice*, believed in the Nazi's twisted ideology and propaganda. Some people, again including the *Milice*, were anti-Semitic and actively turned in Jews to the Gestapo or helped round them up. Some people willingly divulged information about the underground. Uncle Émile spent time in prison because a neighbor told the police he listened to the BBC.

Some women liked, or even fell in love with, German men. Uncle Émile and Aunt Suzanne's own daughter, my Cousin Paulette, had a serious affair with a German civilian. Many people amassed wealth by dealing with the German authorities and businesses. Some believed Hitler would win the war, therefore why not stand on the Nazis' side and prepare for a rosy future in their "New Europe." With France having fallen into political chaos, some people despised French slothfulness and appreciated German order and discipline. The emotional power of the German victory also was an aphrodisiac for some lost spirits. In the Nazi ideology, they found the strength they lacked in themselves.

Some actively sided with the Nazis in their hatred of French communists and Russian "Bolshevism." Ignorance also was a factor that swayed some—these people believed only in what was officially printed and didn't have the ability to read between the lines. And there were many who were blackmailed into collaboration by the Gestapo.

Living during a war is disorder—of that we'd had plenty—but included now, too, was disorder of the mind. Accustomed values were thrown to the wind. Some attitudes that before the war would've been considered wrong now were acceptable and worthy of praise. The shady *filon*, or "know-how," was now the catchword. If you didn't have it, you'd starve and be beaten in the survival game by the Germans and even some of our own countrymen.

Indeed, we helped each other to cope, but at the same time remained extremely careful about who we assisted and in what form. We chose our friends well. Suspicion prevailed everywhere. The simplest activity or slightest acquisition was kept secret. If we had a pound of butter, we hid it, even from relatives. If we had two pounds, we shared with one of them. They in turn kept it a secret from everyone else. It was an extraordinary game, somewhat like children playing hide and seek. We spoke in whispers, because the "fifth column" was listening everywhere. The German response to violations proved so erratic that no matter how small our infractions, we always kept them secret.

The Blackout

The Germans strictly enforced the blackout. They directed us to hang heavy cloths or blankets in windows at night to keep light emissions from revealing the positions of buildings and streets to enemy observers. The Royal Air Force was becoming more active, with bombings more frequent, mainly at night. Depending on their mood, the German night patrols might send blackout violators to a concentration camp, or simply reprimand people, reminding them to take more care.

One winter evening in 1943, Madeleine Kronemaker, grandmother, mother, and I sat around the table visiting. At about 8 p.m., we heard "the boots" coming up the stairs! We were terribly frightened. Madeleine's face grew ever so white, even green. Unbelievably, grandmother remained silent. So did I. Mother surprised us with her courage; she stood up, poised for the doorbell to ring.

When it rang, she opened the door. There stood two Germans. One spoke in an arrogant, commanding voice we couldn't understand. The other came into the room, and pointed at a small gap in the blackout cloth that let out light, which we hadn't noticed. Mother said she was sorry, and fixed it. The first soldier spoke a lot, and angrily. We became even more afraid, if that was possible.

They talked to each other, and the more arrogant one looked into the kitchen. We'd heard how they searched houses, opening everything, looking under mattresses, spilling drawers, taking what they wanted, and breaking what wasn't to their taste. I was especially frightened because I'd started making the flags of the Allies—Russian, British, American, and French—out of old sheets. They were hidden between the mattress and springs of my bed. The Russian and French flags were finished, and the stripes were cut for the American banner. If they found these, we were in deep trouble.

But God saved us—literally. At the beginning of the war, the church offered to install a picture of Jesus in the home of each parishioner. The priest hung it with ceremony, and blessed each house. We weren't to move the portrait, so it hung in our dining room. The gentler German noticed it, making the sign of the cross—Lo, a Catholic! How we prayed silently. My grandmother crossed herself. The two Germans talked to each other again, said something to us, clicked their heels, and left.

We sat there sobbing, and repeating over and over, "Thank you, Jesus, thank you, God." Mrs. Kronemaker dashed to check on her sleeping child, then told us that she'd turned sick to her stomach when the Germans came up.

A few minutes later, Mrs. Guissiani called to us from downstairs—her legs were wobbly from fright, she couldn't walk up. She'd heard the Germans stomping up the stairs. She was especially frightened because she and her husband were listening to the BBC. Furthermore, they had counterfeit coupons in their apartment—quite a lot of them—to be passed on to the underground. Even though Mr. Guissiani had had a taste of prison, it didn't stop his involvement in the underground. Through his fellow Italians, he was determined to carry on, no matter what the cost. When sure that no Germans were in the neighborhood, Mr. Guissiani went to the garden by himself to dig a hole and bury the coupons. No one else was to know where, not even his wife.

We prayed some more, practically all night, and also took a drink of fierce alcohol. We didn't go to bed that night. Mother refreshed her makeup and went to work at 7 a.m. as usual.

We were especially thankful that grandmother was with us. I cannot say what her contribution was, but it was enough that she was there. To us, she was a symbol of strength. She was our spirit. Her prayers, we were sure, had more power than ours.

During the RAF raids, the Germans sounded the air raid alarm for civilians just as the planes were overhead—on purpose, I suppose, giving us little or no time to get to bomb shelters. I found out later that the Germans had their own signal, but the RAF warned us themselves.

It was an eerie sound—about 10 minutes before the British bombed an area, a RAF fighter plane equipped with sirens would fly over, giving warning of the approaching bombers. When hearing this, we knew to go to our basement shelter, as occurred one evening when the RAF bombed Lunneville and some close-by German munitions storage.

One afternoon around 3 p.m., we heard the same eerie sound and saw a plane circling. This was an unusual daylight raid; I didn't go to the shelter because I wanted to see what was happening. We saw a group of planes over the Villers neighborhood just to the west. It was astounding; we couldn't keep our eyes off them. Near the top of the hill stood the Château de Villers, an old, large farm with turrets on both sides—a beautiful place. Before the war I used to go there to see the peacocks in the yard.

One plane came down, dropping explosives and blowing off the left side of the château. Other planes followed, with other bombs shearing off parts of the château until it disappeared. No misses, no mistakes—a perfect job! But German fighters gave chase. We saw two English planes go down, and one German. It was exciting to see them fighting, but very sad also. One pilot floated down in a parachute; we didn't know if he was German or British.

Most of the people on my street watched from the sidewalks. As the planes began fighting, pieces of whistling metal started falling in our locality. A fragment about 3 x 4 inches broke through a window and landed in our hallway—we'd seen enough! We went back in.

Later that evening, we heard that the château served as the German headquarters for the region. A coup to the *Résistance*; they'd pinpointed the target perfectly for the RAF. Whether gossip or tales, some people said the château's owner, ousted by the Germans, had provided the information himself. Like so many other things, this couldn't be proved, and only remains in a few memories today.

Though the château stood just a few hundred yards from Villers, not one house or person in the community itself was touched during the bombing. The RAF was to be commended for its accuracy. Only one French person died, our newspaper delivery woman, an elderly lady who apparently was searching for mushrooms near the château. We mourned for her, but also were pleased that there hadn't been other deaths. We felt it was a miracle.

My First Job

Now 15, with no hope of becoming a novice and entering the convent, I lost interest in the Sacré Coeur school. I did little for a few months, other than help mother at home and some with her work. Mostly I visited friends. That fall, mother insisted either I return to school or find a job. I still took diction and drama classes at the conservatory, but mother said this didn't have a future—meaning it wouldn't get me a paying job.

Aunt Suzanne in her commanding way still held the power in the family; she was sending her daughter Paulette to the Jammerais Buffereau, a secretarial school. This would be my next endeavor. No argument, I had to go!—as did Cousin Gilberte. However, Gilberte rebelled, insisting that if she had to do as we all did, she'd go to the conservatory as I did. But Gilberte and I continued for the term, until placed in a job. This was a happy time for both of us. Aunt Suzanne's daughter, Paulette, however, quit after a couple of months.

Even our cousin Louisette had to attend the Jammerais Buffereau! I should mention Louisette since she greatly influenced my life for a few months. In those Puritan times (as they appear today), families kept some secrets so padlocked that even their curious children couldn't penetrate them. We suspected the worst of family sins regarding Louisette, when actually very little if anything was an actual embarrassment. First, I was told not to ask questions about her, then told that her dying mother, Jeannette, was a friend of the family, and then that Louisette

Jammerais Buffereau—the secretarial school.

was vaguely a niece. Somehow I knew that Aunt Alice had some involvement, as Louisette was closest to her.

(Many years later, I discovered the secrets about Louisette were very simple. The biggest secret regarded Louisette's mother, Jeannette, and my Aunt Alice. I learned that Aunt Alice had been married and divorced before marrying my uncle Charles. From her first marriage, Aunt Alice had a daughter—Jeannette. She had grown up and got married. It was Jeannette who was Louisette's mother! We were twin cousins!)

Louisette, when I met her, was a little younger than me. She came to the secretarial school and we discovered each other. She loved dance and theater. Whatever one of us said, the other said "amen." Why were we kept apart all these years? Mother was so glad that we saw a lot of each other since she wanted to help, as Louisette's mother, Jeannette, was hospitalized with TB. I brought Louisette home to meet my friends. We went everywhere together.

My grandmother kept warning us, "Watch it, she is a spoiled child," but I was used to that kind of grandmother talk. To all grandmothers, we were too young for makeup, cafés, boys, and everything fun. Little alarming things, however, began to happen. First, a boyfriend at the time, Gildo, told me to wipe my makeup off or his mother would forbid him to see me. Then the priest got into it, telling me to remove my lipstick before coming into the church. Gilberte felt slighted, as I didn't have time to see her anymore. The director of the secretarial school called me into her office, not to question my work or attitude, but to point out Louisette's poor grades, poor manners, excessive makeup, etc. I was angry and shocked.

Becoming aware of these problems at school, Louisette began to feign fainting spells in class. She was dismissed. She didn't want to continue living with Aunt Alice, therefore she came to stay at our house. That did it! My girlfriends soon cornered me, saying they were losing their boyfriends to her. Louisette was absolutely beautiful. Though younger than me, she looked about 18, and acted so. Not one inch of her was less than perfect. I defended her, lost friends, and thought I was losing mother's affection. But I did all the work at home, like Cinderella, when Louisette went out. I wasn't the pretty one; Louisette was taking all the princes. This I began noticing with concern.

Things came to a head one evening as Louisette went over bounds. We shared the same bed, so we talked a lot at night, but I was becoming weary of her and the talk of boys and love. She said things that made me feel uneasy. That night she wanted to show me, rather than telling, and she went a little too far. I got up, went to my mother, and made an ultimatum—Louisette or me! The next day Louisette left.

She was a lovely, affectionate, and actually quite innocent girl, who was very lonely and frightened about losing her mother. I've always been sorry for being so straight-laced, and yes, I must admit, being jealous. I saw her only a few times afterward. Her mother died, her father left Nancy, and we lost touch. Many years later, Louisette visited my mother. By then, she had a wealthy husband and was the mother of several small children. She was doing very well. I'm glad. I'd lost track of her whereabouts, but I am sure she was a beautiful woman as well as a most sensitive one.

In nine months I completed my courses and was ready for placement, which the school guaranteed. We continued attending classes until finding a suitable job. I refused the first offer as an aide-secretary (probably errand girl) to a lawyer. The job was acceptable, but not the lawyer, who appeared much, much too friendly.

I very much wanted the second opportunity, but it didn't work out. I took the entrance examination for a secretarial position at the Crédit Lyonnais, a large French bank, but was told to come back two years later when I'd be 18. I was extremely disappointed.

My next interview proved successful—at Maison Jacob's, Buromodel, an office supply business located downtown on Rue Saint-Dizier. I dressed my best, put my most lady-like foot forward, and went in. I felt crestfallen, however, when the first thing they asked was for me to take dictation. That part was fine, but then I'd have to type it up. I typed well, but slowly. I was afraid this could be my downfall. Next they gave me some journals to look at, some materials to enter. Great, I was good at that. Could I use the mimeograph machine? Yes, if someone showed me how! Did I like to decorate windows? I'd love to!

Another applicant went through the same routine with me. Being a good Christian, I prayed for her, but hoped I'd get the job. I liked Mr. Jacob, the boss. I liked Madame Suzanne Lucienne, the bookkeeper, and Madame Germaine, the typist. I also met three men—Louis, Lucien, and Mr. Walter. Everything looked great. We were told to return the next day. They would choose and tell us then.

When I arrived the next morning, they told us they'd decided to take me. I was so glad. They showed me around, gave me a desk, a big book, a stack of checks to enter, a pile of bills, and a checkbook. Some people came in; I was to talk to them until Mr. Jacob was ready for them in his office. A typist they didn't need. Good!

It was a bookkeeper they wanted, since Madame Lucienne was extremely busy and they'd been falling behind in their work because of the time diverted to greeting people. Mr. Jacob needed someone to "waste" time with clients while he was busy. I was fairly accurate in assessing my skills—I wasn't a good typist, but patient with book work, and a good talker. I hadn't pretended knowing how to use the mimeograph, which was a good thing. Their machine was the only one of its kind in Nancy. They knew I couldn't possibly know how to operate it.

I became the pet of the office. I enjoyed everything; well almost everything—the pay was very low. I learned so much, and found much affection. Mr. Jacob was pleased with me and began using me for tasks involving considerable responsibility. Maison Jacob sold all sorts of paper, office furniture, filing cabinets, calculators, typewriters, and other wholesale items.

Due to the shortage of new supplies and equipment during these times, they also repaired office machines, with Mr. Walter serving as the repairman. In addition, they operated a retail store selling just about any office needs, from pencils to desks. With my window setting, I'd be the sales girl, and I loved it! My only qualm was in dealing with German customers—I disliked them so. Madame Suzanne Lucienne or Mr. Jacob, if he was able, tried to relieve me when seeing them come in.

One particular time, a German general walked in with an aide who spoke French. The general didn't speak a word in French. The general wanted a fountain pen and I showed him several, which he tried. I was happy about the one he bought, which I kept praising as the best. It leaked when full! I'd done a good job of sabotage.

One particular task I took pride in, but which also worried me a little, was carrying cash and checks to deposit at the bank, all concealed in a purse I'd made from mother's stash of velvet and other cloth. Our office felt theft was less likely when an unassuming young person carried large amounts of money in her *zazou* purse than if carried by an older adult. This suited me fine. I was to take my time, use different routes, and loiter around so it wouldn't look obvious that I was going to the bank.

I found much enjoyment in this job and remained there for six months. I would've remained longer if it hadn't been for the low pay.

One day, while on lunch break from work and passing over the Rue de Mon-Désert bridge, I noticed people waving and shouting. I looked down—a long train bearing red crosses on the top of the cars stood on the tracks, full of Canadian and Australian prisoners of war.

Cécile and Nicole's Work Associates

Brown's Furrier—
Mr. Brown *(Jewish; disappeared)*

Frank's Furrier—
Mr. Frank *(Jewish; badly mistreated in prison camp; died a few months after returning)*
Mrs. Frank *(non-Jewish; not taken by Gestapo)*
Mr. Lucien *(sent to German forced labor)*

Gasser's Furrier— *(non-Jewish; friends of grandmother)*

Grundfelt's Furrier—
Mr. & Mrs. Grundfelt *(Jewish elderly couple & daughter; never returned from concentration camp)*

Jacob's Office Supply—
Mr. Jacob *(son held by Germans)*
Mrs. Germaine *(typist; husband held by Germans)*
Louis
Lucien
Mrs. Suzanne Lucienne *(secretary)*
Mr. Walter *(office equipment repairman)*

Marick's Furrier—
Mr. Marick *(Hungarian Jew; taken by Germans)*

Perception de Vandeuvre (tax office)—
Mr. Thévenet *(boss)*
Ramie *(her French POW fiancé returned with German wife & child)*
Yvonne *(girlfriend of U.S. Seventh Army colonel)*

Some of the Canadians called out for food and water; they were starving. The German guards, holding submachine guns, tried to quiet the crowd, but were outnumbered by several hundred fiercely angry French. As a mass we went to the nearby stores, groceries, cafés, and bakeries, where they gave us all we could carry to throw down to the prisoners. This was one of the most exciting, beautiful moments of the war for me. All these people made a chain, carrying food, with the POWs catching it. The Germans screamed at us, but we didn't care. If they'd opened fire, we would've died happy.

I believe the Germans were about to shoot, but a miracle occurred. An RAF plane flew over very low, sounding the air raid alert. We flattened ourselves on the sidewalks. Several planes followed, and to our horror, they were bombing the railroad. The prisoners yelled with joy, waving from the windows. The RAF, however, dropped small bombs to hit a few cars at the end of the train, which exploded like a fireworks factory. This was no surprise; we knew that the Germans attached ammunition cars to Red Cross trains carrying POWs or their own wounded troops.

One plane machine-gunned the side of the tracks. We saw German soldiers fall, but didn't see any of the POWs getting hit. No French people appeared hurt either—incredible with such a mob. We went home commending the English again and thanking God. I went back to my office. My lunch hour was over, but we did little work as I had to tell the tale.

This gave us hope in Nancy. We felt terribly sorry for those POWs, but we were accustomed to the Germans holding prisoners. Our hopes focused on why those Canadians and Australians were here. Where'd they been captured? Halleluiah, some action had happened somewhere! Why didn't the Germans shoot at them or us? Were they becoming afraid of our mob? All good signs. When I first told people what I'd seen, they didn't believe me, but my description of the broad-rimmed Australian hats convinced them. No other army on the surface of the globe wore such hats!

We felt that the British were magnificent for alerting us. Of course, when they attacked, they alerted the Germans as well, who gave them serious chase. Had the RAF not sounded these alerts, they would've lost fewer planes and airmen. During the fall and winter of 1943, these alerts and attacks escalated to almost nightly occurrences, and sometimes several times a night.

Paulette and Walty

I mentioned earlier that one of my cousins became romantically involved with a German. Many German civilians resided in Nancy, including women who arrived to work in offices, join their spouses, or to be with friends stationed there. Most of the men assigned to the nearby military bases, of course, served in the military, but they often enough wore their civilian clothes. The Gestapo people, in particular, dressed as civilians.

Most of the time, we could recognize them because of their attitude, particular clothing, and accent. Their bearing was stiff. And for some reason, they usually wore something green—a color that consequently disappeared from the French wardrobe. We came to despise the color. As for their accent, even those who spoke the best of French retained a somewhat recognizable harshness in tone.

Cousin Paulette became romantically involved with Walty, a German civilian. When Paulette first met Walty, she thought he was French. They saw each other on the tram every day, soon began to talk, and then he asked her for a date. Shortly afterward, she had doubts about him being French, and then he told her he was German. At first she didn't wish to see him, but then they fell in love.

Of course, she tried to hide this from everyone, but couldn't for very long. Walty resided only three blocks or so from Paulette's home, and people saw them together. No one was fooled—he looked German! His hair was cut shorter than most Frenchmen. Besides, few Frenchmen of his age were left in France, so it was fairly obvious. He also made a mistake by wearing a German hat. Paulette asked him not to, but he couldn't see anything wrong with it.

She'd known him for several months before the family heard of it. We'd all been shocked, hoping that her parents wouldn't discover it. Of course they did. Aunt Suzanne tried to make the best of it, but Uncle Émile was crushed. I was absolutely irate about it—Paulette was 18. At the time I was just 15 and, of course, I had no real understanding of love and such things.

To make me feel better, she wanted me to meet Walty and see for myself what a nice person he was. We went to a café, but I refused to shake hands when we met. I didn't speak or answer any of his questions. I had to admit to myself that he seemed decent, nice, but I left. I couldn't sit at the same table with a German. Another time I met him in the street, but moved away even as he apologized for our circumstances.

Before the war ended, Paulette had reason to become very unhappy. Even though Walty suffered from epilepsy—which was the reason he'd been in civilian service rather than the military—he eventually was sent to the Russian front. Paulette was terrified. Walty's brother, a German air force colonel, took her to their home in Germany so she wouldn't suffer at the hands of angry Frenchmen. Paulette eventually returned. They never could marry when the war was over—Walty never came back from Russia.

After time passed and the pain eased for me, I felt sad, and still do when looking back to both of them. I cannot excuse it, but I can understand their feelings.

Style and Clothing

In addition to not wearing any green, other choices in clothing styles became part of our silent opposition. German women wore fairly long skirts; ours shortened in a hurry. Their hairdo was rather short and flat; we let our hair grow as long as possible, piling up our curls as high as we could. They were discrete with makeup; we painted ourselves. We also wore ear rings, as well as the highest heeled shoes we could possibly walk in. The *zazou* look adopted by French youths was the rage!

Dark glasses often were part of *zazou* style, with young men wearing oversize jackets and pipe thin pants. German men had closely shaven heads; Frenchmen let their hair grow much longer than before the occupation, often with well-oiled locks. Men carried canes, and women had umbrellas in the shape of canes—did they feel they were carrying weapons?

We were adorned with the brightest clothing possible. Most women at times wore the colors of the French flag—blue, white, and red—as long as it wasn't so obvious to especially anger the Germans. I made a blue sweater with red sleeves and wore a white blouse underneath. "Swing" music of pre-war American origin also became popular, a perfect haven for rebellion. It was a strong antithesis to the waltzes and polkas favored by the German.

In regard to acquiring new clothing, it really didn't matter how much money anyone had in their wallet, since choices were so limited. When I finally ran out of serviceable shoes, I did have several coupons and enough money to buy a new pair. I went to every shoe store around. The best I could find had *ersatz* tops—not leather, not cloth. No one was quite sure what it was. As with all new shoes at the time, the soles consisted of wood—incredible! But wood soles weren't so bad; at least the heels were high.

Most adults could resort to their old shoes if they hadn't thrown them away before the war. But what about young people whose feet had grown? It was difficult finding adequate footwear, especially since all the good shoe materials had gone to Germany.

Most of us resorted to tailoring our own clothes. I made a cape out of an old blanket; capes were much in style then. One time I felt very lucky when finding some beautiful, red, veil-like fabric in a store. The limit was only one meter (slightly over a yard) per person. I bought it. I then made a blouse out of an old dress, using the new fabric for the sleeves. Fashion called for large sleeves! It was pretty and I wore it a few times.

One day after working for Aunt Suzanne to pay off my debt, I was caught in the rain when bicycling home. It wasn't humorous, as I was tired and wearing my new blouse. But it did get humorous (at least when looking back on this later) when my sleeves melted away in the rain. When getting home, all that was left were some red streaks down my arms. The new synthetic fabric I'd so happily purchased simply dissolved.

The Germans bragged about their discoveries in manufacturing man-made materials—called *ersatz*, a German noun meaning "artificial substitute." They'd "invented" synthetic fuel, which we purchased on the black market; it couldn't even ignite a cigarette lighter. No wonder their vehicles and trucks stalled all over Europe—especially in Russia! This gave us heart.

It was 1943 and many Germans now had long faces. They frowned, and the click of their heels sounded tired. Their arrogance was replaced by meanness. We knew that things were getting better for us when everything became harder for them. An angry German meant a frightened German, which made a Frenchman happy. The shabbier they looked, the happier we were, but in the meantime—we suffered.

The months stretched on, and we became hungrier. The Russians still seemed to be retreating, and dying. But rumors went around, or let's say hope was spreading, that America was doing something.

People were disappearing at an alarming rate. Hostages were taken or killed for the smallest infractions. Mother came home completely shattered after witnessing an incident downtown. When coming out of our vegetable storage place, she noticed a crowd of people and heard some Germans shouting. She went to investigate, but wished she hadn't! A German was kicking a man lying in the street. Another German stood by with a submachine gun, keeping people away.

Shortly after mother arrived, someone went to get a priest, as this was happening behind the St. Sébastien church. The priest arrived and tried to assist the dying man, but the Germans wouldn't let him get close. As the man died, the priest was manhandled by the German guard. Mother left, not able to take it any more. What happened to the priest? We never knew. For several days mother didn't sleep for fear of having nightmares, and didn't eat because she couldn't keep anything down.

When mother stood in the crowd, she asked who the man was and what he'd done. No one really knew for sure, only that he'd said something when the two Germans walked by. It must've been an insult. Bad enough to die? And in such pain? And also to beat up on a priest, who only wanted to provide a few moments of God's grace!

God? Yes, the German soldiers believed in God. Embossed on the belt buckle of their uniforms was the motto *Gott Mit Uns*—"God with Us." Churches were full to the brim with Germans; sometimes I saw them standing out in the street, observing mass, kneeling, and fervently praying. We wondered: What did they pray for? To find better ways to smother all of Europe? Better ways to kill or starve us?

At mass one time, I was so proud of our priest. During the sermon he spoke up about the Jews and their misery. Would we join in a prayer for the Jews who were suffering and dying at the hands of the Nazis? We didn't know how to react! The large congregation timidly looked around at the Germans in the big church, watching in dismay as they stood up and stomped out—all of them. We prayed, but no more for the Jews dying somewhere than for our beloved priest with the courage to speak up—to tell us to have courage, and that God was with him, the Jews, and with us, whether we lived or died. I was ready to give up on my God, but our dear priest told us not to lose faith. I believed in him and tried. But still, the Germans went to church and wore *Gott Mit Uns* on their belt buckles, and people were dying.

My friend Nadine was in distress; she thought maybe her father was a collaborator. Some of my other friends had German lovers, like Cousin Paulette. Mother became so very thin and could hardly sleep. If she dozed off she'd have bad dreams. My father—my dearest father— what was life like for him? His few letters could only say that he loved us. My strong grandmother was always there for us, but so often crying. Mr. Kronemaker was becoming a drunk. Aunt Hélène was in despair over her two sons—Auguste gone to German labor, and Roger whose whereabouts were unknown (he'd joined the U.S. Army in Africa). The Guissiani family was cracking over fear for their absent son, Pierrot, from whom they had no news. A dear friend, René Lunot, was the last stronghold for us all—a police officer, though he appeared to be playing the collaboration game.

I had the hope of the young, but couldn't see clearly in my muddled state. One little ray of hope finally infiltrated into my foggy mind. For me it happened when a friend, Huguette Zint, took me aside, begging me to keep a secret. She had to share it because she was so excited.

De Gaulle and the Americans

Huguette's brother Jean had been in the merchant marine when the war started. The family heard no news about Jean's fate for a long time, until finally receiving a letter from him sent through the underground. He'd been in South America for a while, then joined the Free French army led by Général Charles de Gaulle. He'd also sent a photo of de Gaulle to his family; Huguette showed it to me.

At last I could put a face on that phantom angel so many people were whispering about. What rapture for a hope-starved young woman. With his big nose, de Gaulle didn't really look like a knight as seen in my dreams, but he was close enough to give substance to those dreams.

Jean also had been to New York and Los Angeles, where his ship docked. He was very hopeful that the United States would fully enter the war. I kept this secret dear. America was becoming involved—thank God! We now could hope to be saved.

No words can fully express our joy when first sighting American bombers—B-17 "Flying Fortresses"—high overhead. We counted them, or tried—there were so many we'd lose count. Our joy was overflowing. Today I can't believe that at 16 years old I felt so much pleasure at the thought of those planes dispensing death, but I did—we all did! We were so incredibly unhappy under German occupation; we simply hated them and wanted them eradicated from the face of the earth.

On most days around noontime, B-17s and B-24s flew over Nancy on the way to Germany. We exalted in the powerful sound of their engines filling the sky. They flew in formation—a magnificent sight. Up so very high, they looked like small silver candies shining in the sun— scintillating in our blurring eyes. We prayed for the pilots, and for the success of their missions.

We could see how dangerous it was. German fighters from the base at Essey in northeast Nancy pursued them, and anti-aircraft batteries opened up from all directions. It became terribly noisy in our area; German artillery emplacements stood out in fields from both ends of our street. Sometimes we saw planes getting hit. I saw several fall, with the airmen floating down in parachutes. We prayed that some French person could get to them before the Germans.

A mid-sized American plane fell in a field in front of the Bérin's house near Aunt Suzanne and Uncle Émile's garden in Essey. The Germans arrived first. My aunt and uncle didn't make a move, but other people did. An injured airman could be heard crying in the wreckage. My friend Odette Mangeot spoke English; she lived two houses from the Huguins. With her husband being held prisoner in Germany, she was

Odette and Nicole after the war.

well predisposed to go and try to talk to the injured man. The German guards wouldn't let her get close, but she heard the man asking for water, and help.

She went away, seeking Mr. Bérin, whom she knew worked for the *Résistance*. They formed a plan. The plane had crashed around noon, but they needed to wait until dark to act. They feared the man might die in the meantime, but it was impossible to do anything in daylight.

The Germans probably thought the man had died. They left only two guards at the scene, which is what Mr. Bérin was hoping for.

Odette, a pretty brunette of about 22, dressed up as sexy as she knew how, and set out to visit the German guards. It worked; they became very interested in her advances, while Mr. Bérin and others pulled the injured man from the plane.

The two guards were killed, whether the work of Odette, or some others, we never knew. The next day the Germans conducted a house-to-house search, but, of course, in vain. The underground already had moved the injured airman off to another area. We never heard what became of him.

Mr. Bérin had long been suspected of participating in the *Résistance*, therefore he was the most likely candidate in the neighborhood to be arrested by the Gestapo. He was taken for "interrogation," but didn't come back—ever! After a few days, his devastated family began losing hope for his return. Weeks and months went by—then years. We were fairly certain he didn't "talk," whether the Germans tortured him or not, because no one in his *Résistance* group was ever arrested after this incident. We greatly feared for Odette, who hid out for about a month. When no inquiry was made about her, she returned home to her mother, Madame Duval. Odette later became one of my closest friends before I left for America.

This was the closest I came to this type of activity done by the underground. I knew all the details as they occurred. Not wanting to burden mother with more worry, I didn't mention it until later. It turned out that Aunt Suzanne already told her.

We feared that Walty, being so close to Paulette, might hear of some people who knew what happened. He never said anything about it as far as we could tell. Uncle Émile was a second cousin to Madame Bérin—conclusions could've been drawn by the Gestapo—but apparently weren't.

Marcelle Bérin was so terribly distressed after her husband's arrest. She'd already been extremely worried about their older son, Raymond, who'd left at the start of the war and of whom they had no news (he'd joined the *Résistance*). During this time, Suzanne Bérin and I became close. Previously, she'd told me how rather badly she felt about the hatred burning inside me, saying I overdid it. Poor girl, now she understood completely—losing one's father to the Germans caused the fiercest of hatred! We were sisters in pain. (After the war, the street on which the Bérins lived was renamed for Mr. Bérin, who'd conducted many underground operations.)

Suzanne and her mother had been over for dinner at Aunt Suzanne and Uncle Émile's house when I became involved in a bitter argument with Cousin Paulette. Someone asked if we'd had any news of father? No, we hadn't heard from him for several months. Paulette then said we were making too much of it, that Walty said prisoners were well treated, and so on. I replied: Well maybe OK, but what of reports about camps where Jews and many French people were taken. Paulette said those stories were made up by the *Résistance*. I blew up! I attacked Paulette, who was bigger than me, and we wrestled to the floor. I won't say what I called her! My aunt and uncle were crying. Mother took me home.

It'd been a horrible scene, which hurt the family afterward. Even grandmother wouldn't visit Aunt Suzanne and Uncle Émile's house, even though they listened to the BBC. Paulette's parents lost friends, and many customers. A once proud and prominent family for generations in Essey, the Huguins now had to do their shopping in other parts of town. I'd told Paulette what no one else dared to say, due to their fear of her "friend" Walty. Her father died shortly after the war of kidney failure; some whisper it also was due to a broken heart. Who knows?

Life went on and new hope arose, waiting for news of an Allied landing on the French coast. Another winter was approaching. More people disappeared—more died.

Nancy suffered some from bombings, but not greatly. Our health was adversely impacted, however, because we could hardly sleep and had precious little food. Our nerves were in a terrible jangle. Though we stopped going to air raid shelters, we remained wary whenever planes flew overhead. If we'd constantly gone to the shelters, we would've practically lived in them night and day. At times, only five minutes or less passed between each alert.

Occasionally this proved humorous. One evening, we went to a movie. They had to close down whenever an air raid alert sounded. We simply waited out in the lobby, returning to our seats after the alert ended. After watching just a short time, the alert sounded again. Three times, and the movie was only half over! The manager came on stage, saying he was sorry, but it was too late to continue the film. He joked— "Come back after the war is over."

In the fall of 1943, Nancy had experienced its first heavy bombing. I'd just come home around 6:30 p.m. We heard a dull rumble and looked out, spotting the silver fuselages "twinkling" up high in the late afternoon sunlight. Then the alert sounded—as always, too late. Some German fighter planes went up and air defense guns erupted all around town. The bombers didn't seem to take their regular route. To our surprise, they circled over us. We felt foolish standing in the middle of the street, pretending to be so brave. Finally, we made a dash for the gardens and lay down among the vegetables.

After the planes barely passed directly overhead, we saw many small objects falling down out of the sky. Then shortly, we saw smoky blasts rising in the direction of Essey and Malzéville. Aunt Suzanne and Uncle Émile lived in Essey! We didn't speak—this was us, this was real—we weren't just happily watching the bombers fly by as avengers in Germany. As quickly as they passed over, they were gone. A little later we heard dull rumbling and found out that Lunneville also was bombed.

I rushed to a phone and called Aunt Suzanne—no answer! I borrowed a bicycle—while my mother took mine—and we set off. Yes, it was Essey, and it was bedlam. We couldn't enter by the main streets; the Germans allowed no one in. We took the back routes through alleys.

At first glance, Aunt Suzanne's house appeared to be on fire since so much smoke rose in that direction. The whole street seemed to be a pile of rubble, with firemen and ambulances everywhere. People were crying—some stood around in numbed shock. Uncle Émile and other people were hauling furniture out onto the sidewalk. What little remained of the Denis house next door was burning. My aunt and uncle's residence still stood—with broken windows, and in a ball of smoke—but it wasn't burning. Firemen apparently drowned the blaze.

Four of the five houses across the street were leveled. Nine people had died and about 40 or 50 were critically wounded. The mayor's wife and the grocer were killed; about 100 people suffered mild wounds or burns. Where was my aunt? The Germans allowed Uncle Émile to take his truck to go search for her. Supposedly she was returning from Seichan, a nearby village where they had gardens. Uncle Émile found her, still in the ditch where she'd been hiding during the bombing. People had been killed or hurt around her—she was in shock.

But the attack had been done well. The Essey air base—the planes, runways, buildings, and armaments—were destroyed, plus numerous Germans killed. Later, people said it was a miracle that Essey was mostly spared, being only a few blocks from the airfield. Thousands of people could've been killed. We were in awe of the Americans—that they could bomb with such accuracy. The Germans were taken by surprise, consequently only a few planes went up. The others were destroyed on the ground. Was this because the American planes at first appeared to be

Essey air base after the American bombing.

going straight overhead as they did every day, but then circled back in
about the same direction they had come? At any rate, we were glad the
German's planes were destroyed and they had no time to evacuate the
base.

Almost every day new hope came our way. One night, the eastern
sky glowed red, long past sunset. We wondered what was burning? Later
we heard that Stuttgart in Germany, well over 100 miles east of us, had
been bombed. We felt awe at seeing the sky turn red at such a distance,
but what kind of inferno could cause that? It made us feel uneasy. Was
this not too much? Even for the enemy.

But our conscience about this was put to rest when hearing rumors
about what was happening to the Russians—dying in the millions. And
the death camps? What and where were they? Mr. Kronemaker, working
on the railroad, saw horrible things from his locomotive. He felt sick-
ened when he told us of human corpses thrown out of cattle cars, and
of so many other things we couldn't comprehend. Paris was starving, as
were other large cities. People begged for food in the streets, especially
the elderly and mothers with small children. Yes, the Nazis had to pay
for what they took from us.

As we hoped for liberation, we also felt concern over what would happen when rescue came. Father had told us, "Always keep a supply of fresh water in containers—empty and refill them every week at least—always keep some pétrol for the camp stove for cooking, but especially to boil water—have a first aid kit prepared—and if afraid, have no pride, go hide!"

Like the eventuality of death, however, no one talked much about these things or showed their fear of the future. It seemed almost as if making preparations would bring disaster upon us, but mother and I began discussing it. A little of this was due to father's wishes—we didn't want to let him down.

Mother began accumulating pétrol, getting some on the black market through friends—sometimes a medicine or pop bottle full. We'd have enough to operate our lamp and stove for a few days. I maintained the water jug (about 20 liters)—so heavy to empty and refill.

With pangs of hunger, we looked over the priceless cache of booty I'd bought at the beginning of the war. In my ignorance in those days, I'd made the best choices—chocolate, canned sardines and crab, etc.—nowhere now to be found. No matter how hungry, we didn't touch it. We may have worse times ahead. In fact, we did—the worst was yet to come.

I recall one evening when quietly nibbling a little piece of the small daily ration of bread—three or four mouthfuls. I knew mother had worked all day with nothing to eat. She came home, so happy, with two wrinkled apples from which she hadn't taken a bite. We devoured them with our little pieces of bread. Another time it was walnuts. All we ate for several days were some walnuts and a little bread, but we did so with delight. We had black fingers from shelling the walnuts because no soap was available to clean our hands.

We were so hungry and cold that winter of 1943–44, and couldn't sleep much, even if we didn't worry much about air raids. At night, mother and I huddled in one bed along with my cat Moussy (he survived on vegetable and other table scraps). Despite wearing sweaters, scarves, and gloves, we shivered. The windows iced up to where we couldn't see out. Looking at the beautiful frost patterns made us shiver even more. We thought we couldn't survive another winter like this, but we were wrong—one more was to come. But even when hungry and cold, our hearts were becoming hopeful—the snow and ice eventually began to melt.

Rumors came that the Germans now were having a hard time in Russia. We had a saying: When Hitler visited Napoléon's tomb in Les Invalides in Paris, Napoléon asked him what his plans were?

Hitler said, "I now have most of Europe—I'll take Russia, then England, I will be master of the continent."

Napoléon replied, "Hold it, hold it, not so fast—forget Russia. If I couldn't do it, neither can you. Russia will get you in the end."

Hitler laughed.

We were laughing a little now, and soon hoped to be laughing a lot more.

We noticed a difference in the German soldiers—it wasn't just our imagination! The strong, arrogant, victorious men of earlier years seemed to be replaced by weak, unkempt, older and younger soldiers, rather inoffensive and sometimes almost friendly. Germans soldiers appeared beaten and tired.

American and British planes weren't chased by fighters as they flew over. We saw fewer troops. But the SS was just as fierce, if not more so—we trembled when wondering who was getting shot. More hostages were taken, but also more sabotage occurred. The *Résistance* remained invisible, but their presence was strongly felt around us. Nearly every family had someone, somewhere, who they hoped was doing their duty, if they were still alive. Germans and collaborators were found dead in back streets, empty rooms, and parks, or floating in the Meurthe River. No one asked questions—knowing anything could be a death sentence if interrogated by the Gestapo.

We lived on—depending on hope. Mother continued working as a wholesaler in fruits and vegetables and doing her fur jobs at home for private customers. Mr. Brown, a furrier who mother sometimes did work for, had disappeared. At Frank's fur shop, Madame Frank couldn't endure any more without her husband and quit, and Mr. Lucien had gone to work for a Hungarian furrier, Mr. Marick. Mother did some work for the latter and other finishing at home. (The Germans eventually took Mr. Marick away, like other Jewish shopkeepers. Mr. Lucien went to forced labor.)

This is where I came into the picture again—a young girl could deliver things without being suspect. I'd wear a coat to be delivered and no one was the wiser. Once I wore a mink coat. Someone on the train commented about how beautiful it was. I shrugged, saying, "Oh, it's rabbit—good job isn't it."

I wore a coat of "golden sheep" to Mr. Fleurant's diction lesson. He laughed, saying, "It's not your type." I told him the reason why I wore it. He said in 10 more years I'd be wearing mink. I replied that I'd worn mink last week. "I knew it," he said, "you are precocious."

I haven't worn mink since.

I loved Mr. Fleurant, but why did he try to give me so much confidence? He made me feel like the world stood at my feet with everyone waiting for me—and yet, nothing happened. Where were all the talents and abilities he said I had? He kept encouraging me: Go, do this, do that; yes, you can and will. I tried. He drilled me on Racine, Corneille, and La Fontaine. Yes, I could make tears run down my face doing the lines of Phedre. Yes, I could be a buffoon doing Moliere's *Soubrettes*, but, so what? It didn't get you into the country club. In fact, I would've liked to tell him these emotions we worked so hard at bringing out of me caused more trouble than anything else. I later had difficulty stifling them. He told me to feel, to express! Deep feelings, too, were aroused in me knowing Jews were massacred, the poor were downtrodden, and we were starving. He told me—he forced me—under grueling work. Later when I got to America, I felt like a fish out of water. My husband would say, "Facts, use facts, not emotions."

The war still raged on, but we had hope now, though feeling something had to happen soon because we were cracking up. Even grandmother's spirit was low. She was devoted to trying to feed us the best she could, at times fortunately providing butter, ham, or sausage. Then mother took over my grandmother's business entirely. I kept on working at Maison Jacob. We bided our time.

Grandmother had a difficult time of it—a number of people close to her were collaborators, a few by choice, some out of necessity. One instance of seeming collaboration especially hurt her—René Lunot, a

René Lunot, before the war.

policeman. He was young, my mother's age. Years earlier when he was a child, grandmother had practically helped raise him. Because René's mother worked as a cook for my grandmother, he slept alongside my mother in the cradle when she was a toddler. When they were children, mother and René played together. As they entered adulthood, mother married while René went into the military, serving in Africa. He later returned, married, and joined the police force. Both families remained friends, but we saw little of René.

When the war began, he was assigned as an officer in the African Corps of Sénèngalese—rough shock troops that didn't carry firearms, only knives. Firearms were considered too dangerous for them to handle. They did magnificent work in repelling the Germans, but to no avail. René was badly wounded, but saved by a courageous Sénèngalese who carried René to the rear at the cost of his own life. The Germans often out of hand shot captured Sénèngalese and other French soldiers from Africa. The Nazis treated Blacks about as horrendously as Jews.

René survived, returning to the police force. I saw him directing traffic once. He advanced to police chief. He came by a few times; a good hunter, he brought us some game. He also had mother sew wildcat pelts into the lining of one of his jackets.

Many of us felt badly about René. How could he kowtow to the Germans, playing the cooperative game in a police force taking orders from the Gestapo—and working hand in hand with them? It was difficult. People turned their heads when seeing him. Grandmother was hurt; mother also. His name was no longer mentioned.

Others had a similar fate. Because Mr. Jacob, my boss, sold office supplies to Germans with a smile, his wife left him. His son, a priest, no longer saw him. Mr. Guissiani was called a *sale macaroni*, essentially meaning "dirty Italian." There was much French resentment over

Mussolini allying with Hitler. I defended Mr. Guissiani, as well as Gildo, an Italian youth on our street. Mrs. Guissiani couldn't go out of the house without being insulted by people saying her disappeared son, Pierrot, probably had joined the German army.

Pain, pain, pain—many, many people felt pain. Sometimes the pain had no basis in fact when everyone blamed the Germans for everything, even when unwarranted. The father of a friend of ours died of a heart attack. They blamed the Germans. Mrs. Kronemaker's baby died of "crib death." She blamed the Germans. The little girl was about 15 months old—a little doll. As is the French custom when someone is ill or has died, mother and I took turns watching over her. When standing watch one night, I couldn't take my eyes off the dead little girl. She turned bluish in front of my eyes. When watching alone, I touched her—so cold.

This was my first close experience with death—watching, touching a dead being. In her I saw all these people who were in pain. My faith in God was severely tried—but I didn't completely falter. This child and all the others wouldn't suffer anymore; they now were with God. I had to believe it or lose sanity. God had to be with us. This I knew. I couldn't believe that our God was the same God that the Germans prayed to— impossible! This I've battled for the rest my life.

Of course, not all was pain and anguish. We acquired a philosophy to live by—whenever we could find fun and enjoyment, we took it. We went to the theatre, movies, restaurants, and cafés. A golden era of entertainment was to be enjoyed. We attended plays performed by artists from the *Comédie Française* of Paris. We also saw fine singers and dancers, such as Serge Lifar. After the theatre, we'd go to Chez Walter, a restaurant in Nancy with a good band and where artists gathered after their performances. Those evenings are precious memories.

We often went to the movies. Many of the films were German— those that weren't propaganda were quite good. Some French movies also were excellent. I was a fan of many actors, collecting their photos and autographs that I hung on my bedroom walls.

Many cafés had bands and we'd forget much of our pain when losing ourselves in music. The range extended from Viennese waltzes (to please the Germans) to "swing," which had just come in—and we reveled in it. Jazz was a favorite, as were the songs of Édith Piaf, Tino Rossi, and Charles Trénet (in happy exile in America!). Édith Piaf's *La Seine*, Tino Rossi's *Ave Maria*, and Charles Trénet's *La Mer* made us cry, but we needed this kind of release and needed these kinds of heroes. Bizet's *L'Arlésienne* and *Carmen* were superb for escape, as were concerts at the Salle Poirelle. Because I attended the conservatory, I took great advantage of getting low priced tickets. Mother, Aunt Suzanne, Paulette, and I often went together. If we had our differences, we'd forget them and have a good time.

We discovered a fine little restaurant, whose owner we called *la Chouette*, "the Owl." Mother saw to it that *la Chouette* was supplied with fruits and vegetables and she in turn provided good meat for dinner. A nice arrangement—we ate there often. The first time I got really drunk occurred here when the whole family and some friends celebrated Uncle Émile's birthday. *La Chouette* closed the restaurant, reserving the evening for us. We ate, drank, and sang until long past curfew. As our house was the closest, mother decided that Paulette would come back with us. Poor Mama! Paulette and I were acting very happy. We even accosted some German soldiers. They didn't bother us; in fact, they ran away. When getting home, we became very sick and hung over. I didn't enjoy that feeling at all.

This brings up one point. Though very afraid of German cruelty, women never feared being sexually molested by them—not even being whistled at. Rape was unknown in our city. Girls had no worries in that regard. At least we were free of that, since we had so much more to worry about. The Germans either were well-disciplined by their officers, had willing mistresses, or went to designated brothels. Apparently that was satisfactory.

Our family still gathered as in prewar times—only there were fewer of us, mostly women, with Uncle Émile and Uncle Charles being the only men. We visited on our *Fêtes* (name's day) or simply got together. Uncle Charles frequently fished in the Meurthe River, so we were assured of some food.

This reminds me of an amusing evening with mother after Uncle Charles gave us a package of fish to take home. It was a hot summer day. Still early, we decided to go to the movies. Mother put the package of fish under her seat. We then took a walk in town, with mother carrying the package. We decided to take the tram. When we got on, it was terribly crowded. I'd mentioned to mother shortly before that the fish smelled fairly strong. We laughed—but in the tram it became a nightmare! She stood near a German officer. People began remarking about the odor—maybe it was the German—and etc. Someone said whoever had such a foul object in their possession should be thrown off. The German probably understood French and became very ill at ease. He gave mother dirty, angry looks—he knew she was the source of the offensive smell. She was very embarrassed and almost got off the train. I tried not to appear to be with her—I couldn't help her anyway.

Finally the tram reached our stop—relieved, we stepped off. The fish smelled horrible by now. Mother was ready to faint. I saw a garbage can and threw it in—we felt better. We began to laugh, and couldn't stop. Too bad we lost the fish—we could've eaten well. We just said, *C'est la guerre.*

We laughed about things that wouldn't have been funny in normal times, and we did incongruous things. We visited fortune tellers; they made much money in those days! People wanted to know if their tomorrows would be better. We bought useless things at the flea market—we actually had some money to waste. We couldn't spend it on necessities, so we bought frivolous objects. We generally didn't look to the future, we thought only of the present.

We went to tea shops, drank *ersatz* coffee, ate ice cream made of skim milk, used saccharine, and consumed cookies made of...we weren't sure of what! If the French had sinned through their stomachs, they were now paying their expiation. We bicycled all over the countryside to find kind farmers and make exchanges for produce—good exercise for skinny people!

With the coming of spring 1944, we hoped something would happen. We became reckless, harassing the Germans and collaborators as best we could. April 1 is called *Poisson d'Avril*, "April Fish." We tried to pin an April Fish on as many Germans as we could, whether in trams, the stores, or by bumping into them on the streets. It was a silly, small thing, but a strong tonic to frustrated young people.

The people owning the four-story house next to our home were collaborators and had many German guests, usually high ranking officers. (In fact, Germans would be stationed in their garage for a few months before our liberation.) We gave them a bad time. My job was to constantly use our electric gas lighter to produce static whenever they listened to German news on the Stuttgart radio station. It drove them mad. Their maid came out on the balcony next to ours to complain. It was childish, but when one is so helpless, any small action of resistance is necessary to remain sane. These people left for Germany about a month before the liberation. We wished we could've harassed them even more.

How courageous mother was. To feed us, including helping Mrs. Guissiani and Mrs. Kronemaker, she went everywhere she could think of to find food—always on a man's bicycle without brakes. She sometimes rode on a flat tire. To stop or go downhill, she dragged a foot, not easy on a man's bicycle. What was most beautiful—her hair, makeup, and clothing always were perfect, unless she got rained on. No matter what happened, her grooming came first. She said she wouldn't let a German see her without lipstick or mascara—that is what we called French Pride!

D-Day, June 6, 1944

Libération was a word that began appearing in our vocabulary. We'd heard reports about Allied defeats in North Africa. We were told Rommel was victorious. Then came rumors that the Allies actually were the victors. We really didn't know what the exact situation was. The Germans told us England was destroyed by bombing, but then we heard that the Americans were in England in large numbers. We wished to believe the latter. Even more British and American planes flew over on the way to Germany, if that was possible. How we prayed that they wouldn't be shot down.

Spring was near, and then it arrived, but nothing happened! When? We were so tired. We watched the trees bloom, the blossoms fall. When...? It had to happen, we prayed—then it did!

I was at work. My employer, Mr. Jacob, came into the office with a big grin, telling us to take the day off—the Allies had landed in

Normandy! We jumped up, hugged, cried, laughed, and kissed, bursting with joy. I went to find mother and tell her.

I don't remember how Mr. Jacob heard the news, only that he had some affiliation with the underground. Many French townspeople despised him for smiling when dealing with German customers, but his smiles covered up the real story. I couldn't find mother, so I went home, hoping she was there. She was, and she'd heard the news. What a marvelous day! Lots of people already knew about the Allied landing and were smiling. Then everyone grinned as word spread everywhere. What happiness! Tomorrow we'd think about what would or could happen to us in the future, but today we jumped for joy!

The Germans acted as usual, as if nothing had happened, but how smug we felt. What a marvelous feeling!

We had no idea how long we'd have to wait to be freed. Nancy was close to the German border. We knew that the Americans had to cross all of France to get to us. We had no doubts about the coming victory, but how would the Germans behave toward us in the meantime? How much fighting would occur in Nancy? So many questions we couldn't answer. But we were happy—we might die in the liberation, but we'd die happy. That's what we told ourselves. But, of course, we didn't want to die, now that freedom was coming.

Mother and I decided to stay in close contact as much as possible. We'd come home for lunch and return directly home after work. We always told each other where we'd be, and to come home immediately if anything unusual occurred. Time went by—summer came, then passed—long day after long day.

Then there were the German V-1 missiles, and later V-2s, flying over. The Nazis called them "retaliation weapons." In mid June, the Germans first began launching the smaller V-1 cruise missiles, initially aimed mostly at England. Then in the autumn (after the Allied advance on the continent), they began launching the larger V-2 rocket, mostly at England and the Low Countries, but also targeting Paris and some other French cities. Some accidentally went off course, landing in various places in France. We were terrified of these missiles—there was no warning of their coming.

One morning when getting ready to leave for work, I heard a strange noise, much like pots and pans rattling together in a box. As the noise approached closer, a whistling sound was added. I had no idea what the object was, but heard later it was one of these missiles. It exploded in the outskirts of the city. Good thing we could hear it. If one heard it, one was safe; it had passed over.

I hurried to finish the home-made flags lying half-forgotten under my mattress. The American flag was left for last, not because I thought it didn't deserve a better place in line, but because I had difficulties with the stars—two problems. First, I didn't know how many stars there were on the U.S. flag. When asking a friend, she told me there were 48. I was aghast. I'd completed about a dozen, but they were too large—no more room to fit them on the flag. I cut smaller ones, but my second problem was sewing them on. I ran out of thread; more thread was impossible to find. I gave up and just sewed on as many as I could. I ironed the flags and carefully placed them back under the mattress, hoping it wouldn't be long before I could take them out.

Sticks to which the banners would be attached had to be found. At night—to avoid the Germans patrolling our street from seeing me—I cut branches from bushes in the backyard. I was ready. Many women were busy in those days making Allied flags out of old sheets and other cloth scraps; stores ran out of red and blue dye months before.

How I wish I'd kept those flags, but I will always have them in memory.

Libération

September came and the Americans were finally getting close. Our next few days were feverish with excitement and fear. We were completely cut off from the outside world with no real idea of what to expect. The Germans appeared to be in the same mode, just sitting there, waiting. They were calm, playing cards on the sidewalk or just talking to each other. They ignored us and we them.

Afraid to go to sleep, Mother and I took turns staying up. As babies are usually born at night (or so we think), so must the rebirth of freedom. The next few days went by uneventful, but as night came, our hearts beat faster when hearing every distant sound with the hope that it might be the Americans. It, the big it—what would it be like? With this in mind, we decided along with the Guissianis and Kronemakers that the time had come to lock the front door and get ready to use our shelter in the basement.

I replenished the water supply. We checked our alcohol, stove, and light, our meager food supply, our most valuable possessions and papers. Mattresses and blankets were laid on the floor of the shelter. We were ready. One night we decided we would sleep there. Why? I really don't know! Everything was so normal, so peaceful—the ominous calm before a storm.

The first American artillery shell exploded that night about two blocks from our house. There were German gun emplacements in our neighborhood fields. Then a second landed in a straight line with the first, about 20 feet closer. The third came somewhat closer. Shells kept landing close to the corner of our street—then stopped. Since nothing seemed to be happening, we decided to lie down and go to sleep.

In the night, Mr. Guissiani had to relieve himself; he tiptoed to the back door, probably afraid to go upstairs to use the bathroom. He woke us up when banging his head against the washtub. When outside—a blinding light, an explosion, and Mr. Guissiani ran back inside, having barely relieved himself. This shell must've hit in front of our house. Another half dozen fell. Then all quiet again. We tried sleeping a little. The Guissianis' little ones, Jeannot and Gerard, held onto me for dear life.

Coming out the next morning, we found big holes in the street—but little other damage. Only the church roof had a big gap in it. With rain threatening to fall, the priest asked Mr. Guissiani to see if he could make a quick repair job. Mr. Zint went with him. They took their shoes off before walking on the church roof and got to work. Around noon shells began hitting again—in the same places, and from the same direction. Mr. Guissiani and Mr. Zint ran back home in their socks at a speed no one would've thought possible. We laughed, but not much. We went back to the basement.

That night, the same thing. This time we took a relief can with us. My cat, Moussy, didn't like sharing my mattress with the children. He snuggled in with mother who slept alone.

The next day was a little different as the Germans looked busy. Traffic picked up. Tanks and all sorts of vehicles moved along the Rue de Villers. Many Germans walked by in their full gear. There was no singing or fancy marching, just fast walking. We knew something was happening; it might not be very good for us with this horde of Germans now around us. The shelling didn't recur. The church roof was almost covered, thanks to Mr. Guissiani drafting every capable person to cut lumber and use a hammer. The rain held off. Cannon fire and some- times the sound of machine guns were heard in the distance, but not enough to please us.

By late afternoon, German vehicles hauled off the artillery stationed at the corners of the street. Was this a good sign? Also, soldiers billeted in nearby garages, including right next door, appeared to be packing up their vehicles. As we watched them from our windows, we felt fairly happy, though also quite uneasy.

Mrs. Guissiani called us all downstairs, saying one of the German soldiers she knew had come to see her. Speaking good French, he told her they were leaving, and apologized if they'd troubled us. I think he meant much more than just the fact that he'd been staying next door. He left a bag of walnuts for all of us, since he couldn't take them with him and knew we were hungry. We were somewhat touched by this gesture and felt slightly guilty for not enjoying them. But our distrust was such that we all agreed to throw the nuts away. We couldn't take a chance on them being poisoned. This encapsulated my last feelings of the average German in the occupation—a sense of deep distrust, and of sorrow, too.

The soldier also told Mrs. Guissiani that we should remain in our shelter for the next few days and not come out for any reason whatso- ever. The main troops were pulling out to the *forêt de Haye*, but the SS were behind. Though the regular *Wehrmacht* soldiers had no intention of harming civilians, he couldn't speak for the SS troops. We should be wary and prepared. We believed him and went to the basement after warning our neighbors, who also barricaded themselves. We knew that when we next came out, we'd be free.

We had no firearms, but with our sharpest knives and hatchets handy, we stood ready. Our lamp was quite useful. During the after- noon, the Germans cut off gas, water, and electricity. I remembered my father's voice four years before when telling us to prepare for such an eventuality.

By nightfall, the German traffic thinned and the neighborhood became fairly quiet. We remained wary that they might've left time bombs, such as in the garages where they'd stayed, but nothing happened. We hoped and prayed as never before—openly. We had no bravado left and no longer hid our fears. We didn't even pretend that we wished to lie down—we were fluttering with joy, anticipation, and fear. We prayed, talked and prayed some more, and waited.

At times, everyone fell quiet in unison, listening. But no sound, except the rumbling of distant artillery. Around midnight, we finally heard something and froze in fright. Someone was banging on the front door. We remained as quiet as possible, breathless.

More tapping—then the sound of a breaking window! Picking up their pitiful weapons, Mr. Guissiani and Mr. Kronemaker stood at the foot of the stairs on each side, with hatchets in one hand and knives in the other. The children huddled.

It happened so fast, I'm not sure I felt any reaction. One, two, several men with rifles under their arms, revolvers in the other hand, broke the door open and tramped down the stairs. One man took off his head covering and cried, "Mother, Father!" It was Pierrot Guissiani!

Mr. and Mrs. Guissiani screamed, smothering him in a huddle—his sister and brothers likewise clung to him. The scene can't be described. Pierrot finally managed to pull away—he had work to do. He said he'd be back in a few days. He and his companions took great risk in coming, but Pierrot had to see his parents after being apart for so many years.

He also wanted us to be armed. He left rifles and ammunition. After quickly kissing his parents, he and his companions left to continue with their assignment, clearing Germans out of Nancy and assisting in the arrival of the Americans.

Mr. and Mrs. Guissiani sobbed in each other's arms. Their son was alive, he wasn't an escaped traitor, he was doing his duty for France. So happy, we forgot our fear for awhile. My friend had come back in all his glory. Pierrot was a man now—a hero in our eyes. He and his companions wore *FFI* armbands—*Forces Françaises de l'Intérieur*—"French Forces of the Interior."

We trembled with joy, but the sound of nearby gunfire quickly quieted us. Mr. Guissiani, still wiping tears, sat on the top steps, gun in hand, ready to protect us. Mr. Kronemaker was by the backdoor. We huddled again. The children, awed by their brother, couldn't stop whispering to each other. Gerard, too young to have known Pierrot, kept asking questions.

We waited, looking at a slit in the window, yearning for the first light of day. We heard intermittent gunfire. As far as we could tell from our muffled shelter, it wasn't very close. Dawn was almost here; we could barely see our hands in front of our faces. Then came full daylight; we could see each other. This morning, September 16, would prove memorable.

It remained incredibly quiet in our neighborhood, though artillery rumbled in the distance. We heard nothing close by except the rooster crowing in the chicken coop, followed by an answering crow. Mr. Guissiani, gun in hand, opened the door up the stairs, went to the front entrance, and then came back, saying he couldn't see anyone, anywhere. Then he and Mr. Kronemaker cautiously walked into the street. Mr. Zint likewise came out. We also went up.

Neighbors were looking out their doors or windows. Everyone asked if others were alright; did anyone know anything? They'd heard a noise during the night—a window breaking. The Guissianis proudly replied, "It was Pierrot. We didn't open the door so he broke in." The neighbors said they knew Pierrot was loyal all along, such a good boy! We forgot some of their previous remarks. Things like that are dismissed when one is smothered in happiness.

We all went back indoors, for it surely wasn't safe to stick our noses out. Pierrot had warned us. At about 8 a.m., we took another look outside. Still no sign of anything happening. With hope and pride renewed, Mr. Guissiani now felt no fear. He got on his bicycle, with gun at the ready, and left for a longer look, joined by Mr. Kronemaker and a couple of others.

It seemed we waited hours for them to return, when in reality it was only a half-hour or so. When coming back, they didn't exclaim out loudly, but simply said, "The Americans are in town."

No one shouted, we only looked at each other, eyes brimming with joy, and then went up to our apartments, full of purpose. We had much to do—living started again. My first act was to put my flags out on the balcony. I noticed others doing the same. We waved at each other, giving the V for Victory sign with our fingers.

We dressed up in red, white, and blue, and put on our Cross of Lorraine pins, proud that Joan of Arc's cross was the Free French symbol on the French flag. Mother made herself up as beautifully as she knew how. When passing in the street, we gave others little hugs or a quick kiss. We felt too emotional to speak. The cheering would start later.

Mother said, "Stay here, I have to go see for myself. I'll be right back." She left on her bicycle, pert and pretty, her hair looking as if she'd just stepped out of a beauty shop, and wearing "our" one pair of good stockings, saved for the biggest day of our lives. I watched her leave. Everyone was on their balcony or out in the street. Some shouted to her, "Be careful, Cécile." I was so proud of her. I knew she wanted to go to grandmother's house.

I, too, was itching to "go see" for myself. I went and caressed the flags, not knowing which I liked best. My heart overflowed for all of them. All four of them!

Americans entering Nancy, September 1944.

Joyous crowds met the American tanks. The man to the right wears an *FFI* armband.

I went to our precious cache of delicacies. This was the time. I picked out a chocolate bar and began eating. Victory! This was truly it; we were saved. I opened a can of sardines and called Moussy, our indoor cat. He wasn't far and must've smelled it. He might've known he was saved too. He wouldn't be snatched to become someone's "rabbit stew."

Gunfire could now be heard. Artillery shells constantly fell on the hills to the north, but who cared—we had wings—what sweet music it was. A group of us couldn't wait any longer. We went downtown. At Place du Bon Coin, a vast group of people had gathered, looking toward Rue du Sergent Blandan. Now a roar of cheers began.

Some strange little vehicles were coming up the street, followed by tanks. The mass of people moved as one body, I in the midst. The vehicles stopped, unable to move forward an inch. We swarmed around what we later learned were jeeps. We kissed, hugged, loved, and adored the GIs in these vehicles.

We screamed, cried, whispered, "Thank you, we love you; thank you, and thank you God." We crossed ourselves, we kissed them some more, and gave them flowers which we'd snatched somewhere. The American soldiers smiled and hugged back, overwhelmed. The dried mud and dirt on their uniforms were pure gold dust. Their sweat and grime the perfume of heaven.

We couldn't scream or shout loud enough to express what we felt. For a golden day, our joy was the purest of our lives. No cloud could cast a shadow on this free land. Vercingetorix was adding his battle cry, as he did against the ancient Romans! Joan of Arc stood by us in her gleaming armor, gently smiling, holding a French flag. Napoléon looked happy, too. All of them were with us, saying "Thank you."

Songs of all kinds arose amidst the uproar—the *Marseillaise*, some American songs, the communist and socialist's *Internationale*, and more. We were alive again. We were free. Thank you.

I would've liked to kiss the Americans all over again, but we had to share them. Everyone had to have their part of joy in saying thank you. Besides, the Americans indicated they must move on. We could be patient now and let them go; there were more where they came from. The huge tanks noisily clanked on.

A little further, they were stopped again. Having crossed practically all of France, liberating many towns, I suppose they were used to this. We weren't. This was our moment. We had to see and touch them to be sure we weren't dreaming. We screamed and sang to wake ourselves up from occupation. I'd forgotten what it was like to look forward to the next day, hour, or even moment without feeling heaviness in the pit of my stomach, wondering with dread how I could go on.

We now had wings on our feet. Dreams, ambitions, everything could now come true. In one morning, we could see a whole new life unfolding—full of laughter, fathers returning home, the sun shining, jazz music, and no sound of boots in the night—and maybe even some food!

I now felt I'd better go home. Mother might be back and maybe I could find something special to eat, even supplementing it with the little bit of coffee I'd hidden. I wanted to shout to everyone that I'd seen and kissed Americans. I wanted so much—no, I didn't want—I had it all.

Mother hadn't arrived yet. I was a little concerned, but not afraid. How could anyone be afraid when the strong Americans were here with their tanks and guns. The streets had a holiday air and we whiffed the smell of cooking as women prepared some of their preciously hoarded food. Windows were open, with the hidden radios turned on. Children ran in the streets—now freed from days without movement or sound. Babies cried—Nancy was alive again!

Once in awhile, we glanced toward the *forêt de Haye* to the northeast where the Americans were shelling German positions in the woods. It was almost difficult to visualize the Germans now—as if they'd been erased from our minds, for this morning, anyway. We wouldn't let them spoil the most beautiful day of our lives.

"Mother holding Moussy."

Moussy slept on the couch, probably dreaming of the sardines filling his stomach. Mother finally came home. What a tale she related!

She'd arrived downtown just in time for the uproar. Nancy's grand main square, Place Stanislas, overflowed with people kissing and hugging the few Americans who'd stopped there. She stood there a few minutes, not able to get near the Americans, when shooting broke out. Everyone dropped down in the square and nearby streets. The

Americans shot back from their tanks toward the extensive city park and zoo, a short distance from the square. There were a few casualties, mother gathered, from the screams heard nearby. Projectiles flew all around. She laid on the pavement, her bicycle over her.

As soon as she could get up and move again, with our one pair of hoarded stockings in shreds, she tried to go north toward Malzéville to grandmother's place. The *FFI* turned her back. Malzéville wasn't free yet; the Germans held out beyond the broad Meurthe River. Her heart sank. All this joy couldn't be shared with the rest of the family. With Germans still in positions in that part of town, it meant that eastern Nancy was still occupied. What a deep disappointment.

She turned back toward home, but was stopped by masses of people greeting the Americans. This hampered the Americans in reaching the part of town where the Germans still held out. Sadly, more civilians were killed this day than during the rest of the war. Feeling so safe with the Americans arriving, they'd forgotten all caution.

The *FFI*, numbering in the hundreds, had paved the way, but couldn't pass beyond the Meurthe bridges, still guarded by the Germans. They blew up one bridge, but the Germans got the *FFI* men when they tried swimming across the river.

Mother heard an announcement—General Patton would arrive at Place Stanislas at 2 p.m. to speak to the population. She was exhausted when returning home. But wanting to be at Place Stanislas at 2 o'clock, we left at noon. It seemed as if most of Nancy—free Nancy, that is—headed there. We walked en masse. There was still a little open space in the crowd when we arrived; we managed to squeeze ourselves in.

Rifle shots and machine gun fire could be heard a block or two away in the direction of St. George and the park, but nothing could stop us. (The Germans would hold out there for several days.) If the American general made the effort to greet us from the city hall balcony, we'd stand there to thank him. We felt charmed—the Germans couldn't take away our joy.

We waited, and sang—more starved to sing the *Marseillaise* than for food. Around 2:30 p.m., people began shouting. We looked up to the balcony where several soldiers stood along with the city mayor. The Americans' uniforms looked different from what we were used to seeing.

We hadn't even known the color of their uniforms, but how marvelous they looked. The mayor, probably introducing Patton, choked up when saying a few words we didn't understand. We quieted; tears ran down our faces. All fell silent.

I don't remember the words spoken by Patton; he made a few comments in French. But it was the sweetest words we'd ever heard. He was our hero. We adored him, we revered him, and he was God incarnate to us. We cheered and cheered until exhaustion took over. Slowly, happily, we left for home. Tomorrow would be another beautiful day, General Patton had promised us that. He said something about the Germans never getting back an inch of ground and soon we'd all be free. We walked home on a cloud—angels carrying us with songs.

Our bodies gave out and we slept and slept, but we also listened now and then—hearing cannon fire and machine guns. No Americans had been seen in our neighborhood yet. The Germans were up the hill from us in the woods, but for the moment we had the word of the general.

The next morning, the 17th, we were groggy, and still starved—no water, gas, or electricity—and no stores were open. It wouldn't have helped anyway because we knew the shops were empty, but we were happy. We would manage, and good times were just around the corner. We rested that day, talked to neighbors, pooled the little food we had, and were simply happy.

I began wondering when the French prisoners might be freed. How I thought about father! Did he know about us—that all was well? That we'd made it? I wanted to shout it out loud enough for him to hear.

September 18

When I arose around 8:30 a.m., mother already was gone, probably seeking news about grandmother and our other relatives. I knew how worried mother was. As I brushed my hair by the kitchen window, a small observation plane with American markings circled low over our neighborhood. People looked out their windows or ran into the street, shouting out greetings. The plane disappeared for a minute or two, then came back, landing in the open grassy area just off our street. We dashed to the field.

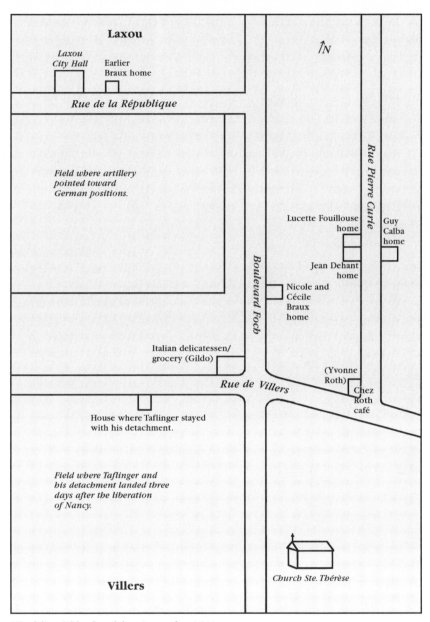

Nicole's neighborhood, late September 1944.

By the time I arrived, holding little Gerard Guissiani in my arms (he couldn't run fast enough), several hundred people converged on the plane. This was the first American to arrive in our part of town, and the first seen by those people who hadn't gone downtown earlier. As we approached, we saw the pilot pacing across the field in a strange way, taking long steps, and apparently unaware of our presence. I learned later he was measuring the length of the landing field.

As I neared the small plane, he was walking back. People mobbed around him, hugging him. When getting nearer, Gerard said he wanted to kiss the "Mezerican," but Gerard became afraid, so I kissed the pilot for him. Everyone who got close enough kissed him. What joy! An elderly gentleman, formally dressed and wearing a Legion of Honor ribbon, greeted him. The moment was touching—no uproar as previously, but a strong feeling of emotion. The pilot's outfit appeared different from the uniforms of the other GIs we'd seen and he didn't carry a weapon in his hands. This American was quiet and gentle looking, simply walking amongst us, smiling.

He climbed back into the plane and we moved off the field, giving him room to lift off. We were sorry to see him leave. I remember telling my friend Huguette that I wished he'd return. I also noted that he had rather small feet.

We stood around for awhile, hoping he'd come back, but as nothing happened, we returned home. We felt truly free now. Only this one American had walked in our neighborhood so far, but all was well. We visited for awhile by our doorsteps.

Around 11 o'clock, our American returned in his small plane! Three other planes followed. Joyfully, people ran and scrambled to greet him again, as well as the other newcomers. They all got their share of love and kisses. I told some people, "Let's go greet our first one again—the one with small feet." We went to him. We wouldn't let him leave again; I certainly was determined not to lose sight of him.

American trucks and equipment arrived that afternoon, along with mechanics, guards, and a cook. This detachment of the Fourteenth Liaison Squadron settled in at an unoccupied house on Rue de Villers, just off the corner from our street. The French occupants had disappeared and Germans lived there for so long that we didn't recall who the

Several of the Fourteenth Liaison Squadron's two dozen or so planes were assigned to the Villers landing field under Lt. Taflinger's command. Note a local farmer's garden in the foreground.

original owners were. A rather large house, it contained a main room with desks, a kitchen, and two bedrooms on the first floor and four above.

Three friends of mine, members of the *FFI*, offered their services and attached themselves to the detachment—Guy Calba and Jean Dehant, 20 and 18 or so years old, and René, another older friend. They kept people away from the planes and also tried, to no avail, to keep young women like me away from the Americans. The first American I spoke to, or I should say I tried to communicate with, was named Daniel, who stood guard by a gate at the field. He was nice and friendly; we understood he was married and had children. He warned us to stay away from the Americans. We wanted anything but that.

Mother still couldn't get in touch with grandmother and came home saddened. That evening, we went for a walk to the field. She simply had to kiss an American; she hadn't had the opportunity yet. She kissed one of the guards and instantly felt better!

Euphoria followed. The Americans now were here en masse. Tanks rumbled along, tearing up the street surfaces when passing. Soldiers threw candies, gum, and chocolate to the children. What a holiday!

I met a sergeant from the detachment, a gentle southerner. He gave us soap, toothpaste, hot chocolate, and strange biscuits called graham crackers. We were so hungry—this was tremendously welcomed.

I and my friends Renée, Huguette Zint, Lucette Fouillouse, Yvonne Roth, Guy Calba, Jean Dehant, René, and the inevitable Micheline Guissiani along with her younger brothers Jeannot and Gerard (who practically lived with me) would virtually invade the Americans' quarters—that is, when the lieutenant in charge wasn't there. Huguette took care of that. She borrowed my book to learn English and told him she needed lessons, etc. He was very sweet and agreed. I wasn't sure I liked that—after all, it was my book. Besides, I felt I had some rights to the lieutenant. Why, I didn't know—he didn't offer me anything, while the sergeant I'd met was so lavish with his gifts.

"Gordon always carried a camera and took this photo of me a day after his arrival."

Several days passed by when Guy Calba asked if I'd bake a cake, because the lieutenant wanted to give a party. Only nice girls, some of the young French men, and the lieutenant's group would be invited. Sure, I'd try. That evening we went— Huguette, Lucette, Yvonne, Renée, myself, and some other girls—and we had a party. We sat around a large table, trying to communicate. Only one person could really do some translating for us—a sergeant of French Canadian origin. But we had a good time. We ate, drank, and laughed at little nothings.

I sat next to the lieutenant, who was the first pilot we'd seen landing at the field. When I asked about the sergeant who'd given me the gifts, the lieutenant said he'd put him on guard duty, which made me sad. He told me not to see this sergeant, but wouldn't say why. I learned later he was married. This was disquieting. The only thing I had with sergeant was that he gave me the best hot chocolate I'd tasted since the war started.

We were young, of course, and the soldiers generally only a little older than us. The evening was delightful. The lieutenant spoke some French, but he and I didn't carry on a real conversation because it wasn't possible. Besides, I thought he drank too much of that fiery liquid called whiskey. I tried a sip; it was like terrible medicine, burning my tongue. Though I was enjoying the evening, eventually I wished to leave. There were some activities among couples. To my surprise, some friends were involved and didn't agree with my principles. I was younger and felt no need for pairing off.

The lieutenant trustingly appealed to the French Canadian sergeant to escort me home. On the way, my problems had only started when the sergeant made advances, but I pared them easily. From then on, we couldn't be real friends, but only rather tolerated each other out of necessity. I didn't plan on a return visit like this one to the American group.

The Germans still occupied Essey and Malzéville to the northeast. Gunfire could be heard day and night; we were terribly concerned about our aunts' families living there, and especially grandmother. The glow of the first few days of liberation now dampened with this worry. Our walls and the windows, taped to prevent them from shattering, shook from the deep rumbling of artillery.

Electricity was restored, but we couldn't drink the water as it hadn't been processed for several days. The Americans were warned, but they drank it anyway. The liaison detachment became victims of the ravages of contaminated water. My friends and I went to visit, only to find men in bed with high fevers and stomach cramps. In fact, many of the troops in Nancy suffered from the onslaught. We were frightened knowing this, since the Germans might return. Had they known, they might've retaken Nancy within hours. It was so sad to see soldiers retching all over town, but nothing could be done. It didn't last long, however—a couple of days and everyone revived.

I decided the time had come to see about returning to work. Only the head secretary was there, Madame Suzanne Lucienne. Yes, she could use a hand. I went back the next day. Of course, our first priority was to have a party. We organized this, and Mr. Jacob laid out a plan for the future now that the Germans were gone and no longer taking all our inventory. What a delight to listen to his dreams. Mr. Jacob's son, Madame Germaine's husband, and my father would return from German camps and the world would be so beautiful again, like six years ago.

We now fully realized how wonderful life had been before the war. How beautiful Nancy was without the sound of German boots striking the sidewalks. How sweet the city smelled without the soldiers' pungent sweet and sour aroma. How comfortable the trams were when our enemies didn't order us to get off to make space for themselves. How wonderful when German troops weren't marching or goose stepping and singing their barbaric victory songs. How we didn't have to fight back tears when seeing a German harassing someone. How we'd had no reason to feel fear for the next day, or minute! We'd almost forgotten.

Now, the precious ordinary soil under our feet belonged only to us. Thousands of French flags fluttered in ever so many windows. We'd forgotten what it was like to walk proudly with our noses in the air! People now smiled at each other. People talked loudly, freely, and gathered together (groups of more than four were forbidden during the occupation). The trees were so green, the sky so blue. We could think and plan for tomorrow. Our joy was almost boundless with each rediscovery. I say "almost," because we knew so many couldn't share this with us—they'd died for us, so we could live in these happy moments of liberation.

The word *merci* constantly fell on our lips—a thank you. People were overcome with gratitude, stopping Americans everywhere to thank them. During the first few days of the liberation, few Americans walked the streets without lipstick on their faces. This was the best way women knew how to express their overflowing hearts.

Some French people, however, had reason to feel less thankful, including those women who'd consorted with the Germans. If they were found, their heads were shaved by mobs. Few could escape, and some were paraded through the streets in shame. Many American soldiers joined in gleefully. I observed the shaving of a woman in a square where a stand was set up for the procedure. Thus, the "turban" fashion in head-wear became most useful to these women.

Collaborators also were rounded up. Some were put in prison and others immediately executed, or shot after a quick trial, depending on their offense. Much violent horror occurred in the first few days of delirium. The pain of occupation was too fresh to be forgotten. Too many had lost too much not to seek revenge. But no revenge could make up for the loss. Only part of our population was present to enjoy liberation. Where were the others—The disappeared? Those with whereabouts unknown? The prisoners of war? The forced laborers? Most of the young men? Many eventually returned, but few came back with minds and bodies fully intact; most never entirely recovered from suffering in Nazi hands.

Germans still stood across the river. How many civilians would be killed before they were ousted? Why was it so difficult to drive them out? What was the *Résistance* doing? Later it was said that the *FFI* and the Americans did all they could to hold the city center, but couldn't cross the river. The Americans had tanks and other armored vehicles, but the Germans were massed at the bridges and crossings. So we bided our time—a miserable wait. The city was split apart and most everyone had relatives on the other side. But finally it would be done. The Americans went further down the river, found a weak spot, and crossed.

Mother had to return to work, but still tried as often as possible to go to Malzéville—all in vain. But trust my dear grandmother! One evening when we got home from work, there she was! She'd been sitting there, wondering how long it would take for us to arrive. All was well—we were reunited again with our grand old lady, and all her love and wit.

She told me right away to stay away from the American soldiers. Of course I would, I said. An Englishman, maybe, but they weren't coming our way. A Frenchman?—I hadn't thought of that. Free French soldiers

The crowd that gathered to get a glimpse of Général de Gaulle.

also were coming into Nancy. On September 25, our fairy knight, de
Gaulle, would be speaking at the City Hall at 4 p.m. We had the afternoon off from work, and I arrived in the square at 2 o'clock. What a
mob—indescribable! It began raining and turned miserable. Some with
umbrellas couldn't even open them because of the dense packed crowd.

I stood next to my friend Lucette Fouillouse, who lived in our
neighborhood on nearby Pierre Curie street—her parents' house stood
back to back on the block with our home. I was three years younger, so
we'd had little in common during my school days. But now that I was
becoming a young woman, our friendship grew. In France, young people
weren't considered to be "teenagers"; they became adults after leaving
school, dressing and acting accordingly. We both had attended the party
with the Americans. She'd met Arthur Pass, one of the pilots, who spoke
some French. She was seeing him as much as possible, and she planned
to meet him that evening at 6 p.m. We hoped de Gaulle would arrive on
time. By 3 p.m., we were soaked; 4 p.m., no general; 5 p.m., still waiting!

At 5:30, Lucette said she had to leave to meet Arthur. She asked if I'd go with her, as it didn't look good for a girl to enter the Americans' quarters alone. I said I had no one to see there. Lucette replied that I could leave out the back door a few minutes after we arrived.

I still hoped to see de Gaulle. But I was thoroughly soaked. Also, I couldn't find mother; we'd planned to meet on the square. No doubt she'd given up and gone home. Alright, I'd go with Lucette. Besides, I was starved, having had no breakfast or lunch. I hoped mother had found something for us to eat.

We arrived at the Americans' quarters. Lucette, to my dismay, went off with Arthur seeking privacy. I stood alone in a small hallway, in what otherwise appeared to be an empty house. I could see part of the kitchen table, and lo!—a box of graham crackers stood on its corner. No harm, I'd take one (the Americans had so many), and then leave. My wet hair and clothes dripped. I reached for the crackers, but someone was there! The lieutenant, the unit's CO, sat alone on the other side of the table— the first pilot we'd seen a week earlier, and who'd organized the party. He said something—I guessed he invited me to join him.

I sat awhile with him, eating crackers. He offered something creamy and gooey (it was peanut butter, unknown to me). I put some in my mouth. Incredible—it stunk and tasted terrible! I sat there barely able to swallow, very embarrassed, so wet from the rain, and feeling ugly with my makeup washed off. The lieutenant said other things I couldn't understand.

When I told him I needed to leave, he kissed me, and removed my wet coat. He got some towels, dried my hair, and found a change of clothes— one of his shirts, and socks and shoes. He had small feet for a man, which I'd noticed before. He then served me coffee, such a treat, and made a peanut butter sandwich, and gave me

Ancel G. Taflinger.

some to take home. He said in French to come back tomorrow. I didn't think I should.

But the next day I went back—and many other days, too! He was Lt. Ancel Gordon Taflinger. When he told me his name, I couldn't pronounce it. In fact, it sounded strange and funny to me. I never could call him "Ancel" as others did—it was too German anyway. I'm not sure what my first nickname for him was, but to me he was "Gordon." When I said my name was Nicole, he called me "Nicky." I was Nicky from then on.

Of course, I didn't mean to come back, especially after noticing some other girls going off in a bedroom with their partners. But I did return for some reason. I didn't think the lieutenant and I would shut the door of a bedroom, and we didn't. But we had a marvelous time trying to communicate; we magically grew extremely close in the following weeks. I learned he'd previously served as a bomber pilot.

As Gordon's French improved, he began asking questions like, "How many children would you want if you get married?" I asked him the same question. We both came up with four. This gave us a strong feeling about where our relationship was heading.

This created a special bond between Lucette and me. She was helplessly in love with Arthur Pass. We'd meet to come home from work at the same time, arriving in our neighborhood at 6:30, and then visit our friends until 8 p.m.—curfew time. This proved to be a problem for me, as mother strictly forbade me to even get near an American. I pretended I was visiting girlfriends or working late—such lies as young women find convenient.

To our sorrow, mother's warning was true—young women often enough weren't safe among American soldiers. A number of GIs ignored their little instruction in how to behave among civilian populations. Practically every day we heard reports, and even read newspaper accounts, about rapes, girls rescued from difficult situations, etc. This was our first disappointment. What we never feared during the German occupation now was a sad fact and difficult to accept. During the occupation, women never had concerns over sexual advances. A knitting needle now went back into my purse and beware to the soldier who pressed too close! I'd meant to use it if a German did, and the same treatment would work on an American, if needed.

Mother finally became suspicious about my whereabouts, so I told her. She said she needed to meet the young man, as custom demanded. Any young man who wished to date a girl had to meet her parents. I brought Gordon to the house. They couldn't communicate, but I knew he didn't meet mother's approval. We left.

When I came home, she said, "No. He's too old." True, he was 12 years older than me and only 5 years younger than mother. "He's too fat"—so unkind and untrue. He was quite slim, but when meeting mother, he wore two sets of clothing—a heavy, leather, fur-lined jacket and pants, all pulled over a regular uniform, plus a flyer's double boots and a helmet over his hat. Plus, he'd had no bath for ages, was unshaven, and mud covered everything. I argued, "How could he look good?" I liked him that way. Besides, he used a magnificent perfume—gasoline.

No matter what mother said, I would visit him. When coming from work, I first glanced toward the landing field, seeing if Gordon's plane was there. After all, we still were at war and these observation planes were involved in the fighting. Some would be shot down during the war or crash on rough landing areas. We could tell which pilot was flying by the individual way they revved the throttle of their engines up and down.

One evening, I didn't see Gordon's plane. I ran to the Americans' house, terribly afraid, but found him there, calm and quiet as usual. Someone else was flying the plane, or something like that.

More than wanting to learn English, which actually I wasn't doing very well (although Gordon was learning French), I realized some-thing else was happening. I had to grow up or lose him. My love notes and poems of the past, just with a peck on the cheek, wouldn't get me anywhere.

Each evening spent at the Americans' quarters seemed like a party, even though we could hear cannon fire. The Germans remained near. My friends Guy Calba and Jean Dehant were regular visitors along with Lucette, Renée, Yvonne, and Raymonde (whose mother kept house for the Americans). The Americans we gathered with included the sergeant I'd met early on (now Renée's friend), Arthur Pass (Lucette's friend), Charlie Leipersock (Yvonne Roth's friend), and Joe (Raymonde's

In the front row (l. to r.) Sgt. Arthur Pass, Guy Calba, Lt. Taflinger, and Jean Dehant, standing with other members of the observation squadron in the backyard of their quarters.

friend), plus Sgt. Norman Noland (from Independence, Missouri, and a nephew of U.S. Vice President Harry Truman), Maurice, Ace, and several others. We usually sat at the kitchen table. These were extremely delightful times!

We'd lose track of the hour—the 8 p.m. curfew came so quickly and the Military Police were strict. After staying too late, which occurred almost every evening, we dashed across the street, hoping the MPs normally stationed at the street corner didn't see us. After getting across, we'd pass through muddy gardens, climb a wall, and jump into more mud and cross other gardens toward home. Guy, Lucette, Renée, and Jean had still further to go, climbing on top of some garages and jumping off into even more mud.

MPs caught Raymonde one evening. She spent the night in jail, but actually enjoyed it. The American MPs fed her strange cakes with holes

Reminiscences of Guy Calba

Guy Calba inspecting a Stinson L-5, accompanied by T/Sgt. Pass and S/Sgt. Noland.

My youth's experiences were quite turbulent during the 1940–44 period. I was born in a Nancy suburb on July 27, 1924. The next year, we moved to Rue du Général Duroc, near Notre Dame de Lourdes. In 1930, my parents built their house on Rue Pierre Curie in Laxou; we moved in on *Ste. Jeanne D'Arc* day, 1931. This house was the second built in the area, in the fields.

A year later, the Dehants moved in across the street. Jean Dehant became my best friend; we attended primary school together. Then, Jean went to the *lycée* Rue des Jardinières, and I to the St. Joseph institute until 1938. In 1939, I entered the Beaux Arts school in the industrial/technical section.

In June 1940, as German troops approached, my father, then head of the ministry for 1914–18 veterans, had the task of evacuating the archives and staff to southern France. He had to leave mother and I behind, unable to tell us his destination as a matter of security. A few days after father's departure, some neighbors with a car offered to take us along to find refuge somewhere in the south.

It took us about three days to reach some friends near Moulin in central France. During the trip, the Italian air force bombed and machine gunned the road. We remained there about five days, but with the Germans approaching again, mother and I took to the road, joining a French military convoy. But after two days of travelling, they abandoned us. Left alone in the countryside, we walked with our suitcases several miles until arriving in a small village called Messières de Cornet, where we took refuge with an elderly couple.

After two months, we at last received news about father through friends in St. Hilaire. We got in touch. Father came to get us and we made our home in an old farmhouse that some farmers allowed us to use. We remained with him for three months, when father regrouped his ministry service in Agen in southwest France. At Agen, we lived in an apartment for a year.

Meanwhile, the Nazis had closed re-entry to Nancy and the province of Lorraine, now under a German governor. Father submitted official requests to return to Nancy, but was refused by the Germans and the Vichy government. He then made the decision to pass his personnel, and mother and I, through the forbidden line with the aid of *passeurs* (persons clandestinely assisting travelers).

Eighteen of us succeeded in reaching the Jura region, south of Lorraine. We'd have to cross the boundary line undetected. On a bright moonlit night, we walked nearly seven miles barefoot (to be quieter) through the fields and forests, stopping now and then when hearing German patrol dogs barking. We stopped in a hay barn in the countryside, resting for a few hours. At daylight, we resumed our trek, in small groups of three or four, until arriving at a country bus stop. Without any difficulty, we boarded a bus taking us to the Besançon train station. From there, we took the fairly lengthy train ride to Nancy.

Our empty home hadn't been requisitioned by the Germans, thanks to Madame Dehant. All these many months, she'd opened and closed the shutters daily, giving the appearance of a family residing there. Through discrete connections, father managed to obtain official papers (identification and ration cards) from the prefecture for us and his personnel, which allowed us to receive ration tickets.

Early in 1942, I returned to the Beaux Arts school, and also enlisted in the "passive defense" for the local neighborhood. Madame Bitch, a dentist, was in charge of the underground in Laxou. She interviewed and studied me, my political ideas, loyalty, etc., and finding me safe, introduced me to Mr. Tollard, a printer on Rue de Maréville in Laxou. In 1943, Mr. Tollard integrated me into the local *Résistance*.

Later, in October 1943, I was put under his direct order until the liberation of Nancy, when I met Lt. Taflinger and his group of pilots, mechanics, and guards. I was a member of the *Forces Françaises de l'Intérieur* (*FFI*),

the overall organization for the tens of thousands of men and women in
Résistance groups across France.

My work in the *Résistance* consisted of delivering or distributing
political "tracts," taking photos of German officers entering or leaving the
kommandantur of the local French *Milice*, and counting the German planes
at the Essey air base and determining their type (transports, reconnaissance
scouts, bombers, etc.). When Essey became a pilot training school with
planeurs (gliders), I also counted their number.

This proved fascinating, but extremely risky. I had the good fortune of
never being suspected. I remained extremely discreet and calm, and, above
all, felt no fear. Friends and family members never knew, or had suspicions,
about my involvement in the *Résistance*.

---

in the center; donuts were unknown in France. This event upset mother
even more.

One evening's experience was frightening. Shortly after I arrived at
the fliers' quarters, an alert sounded and we heard planes coming. The
Americans' anti-aircraft guns, every one of them, opened up in full
force. We huddled in the stairwell, but I was very worried about mother
being alone. Gordon put his leather jacket and helmet on me and we ran
for my house. It wasn't far, but for those few minutes it seemed like a
mile. Flack whistled around us, hitting houses; shells exploded, flash-
ing all over; and the planes rumbled overhead. It was all a mistake; we
later learned these were RAF planes, not German. But for a short time,
it was fearful. I was glad to have returned home. Mother was miserable,
as much in fear for me as for herself. The lights were out, dishes rattled
in the kitchen, and everything shook around us. That evening I learned
something else—with Gordon near, I wasn't afraid of anything. Looking
back now, I see how marvelous it was of him to take me back to mother.

Another occurrence one evening at the Americans' quarters bothered me greatly. The phone rang, someone answered, and then Gordon
abruptly left, not saying anything to me. I waited awhile. Some planes
lifted off, and Gordon didn't return. I couldn't find anyone who spoke
French to inform me about what was happening, so I went home. The
next day I heard that General George Patton wanted a flight somewhere.
Gordon, being his pilot (which, of course, I didn't know), quickly left

"Gordon took this photo of three key American generals—Patton, Bradley, and Eisenhower—while at a landing strip."

without discussing anything with me. I think I forgave him for leaving me so abruptly that evening.

After all, General Patton was our savior, our hero. He almost replaced Joan of Arc for some of us. After the war ended, we were surprised to hear that many Americans felt he wasn't quite the hero he was to us. After four years of occupation, Patton and his troops were our delivering angels. Americans back home, on the other hand, seemed more concerned about his ill-advised comments regarding Allied

leaders, as well as improprieties with some battle fatigued soldiers.
He slapped or roughly treated several soldiers, and was nearly fired by
General Dwight Eisenhower. We thought little of this, as the Germans
had torn off women's breasts and people's fingers to obtain the names
and locations of Jews.

Some criticisms aimed at Patton didn't wash with us. The same
occurred regarding Général de Gaulle. Faults he had—all men have
faults—but few had the determination and ability of these two generals.
Politics and reality aren't always compatible. Our heroes they remained.

I forgave Gordon when hearing the reason for his lack of courtesy
that evening. I only wished I could've seen General Patton up close.
I spotted him a few times in a jeep. We could tell that high-ranking
officers were in a vehicle by their escorts and the pennants on their
vehicle. A fleeting look at them gave us great joy and an immense feeling
of safety. Slowly the Germans were being erased from our mind. Prime
Minister Churchill, too, followed in Patton and de Gaulle's steps to Place
Stanislas.

I saw Gordon every weekday, as well as on Saturday and Sunday
afternoons. I spoke very little English, so we relied on his limited French.
When we couldn't understand each other's words, we looked at each
other, clung together, and tried again. Week by week, our relationship
grew ever so closer in an unbreakable bond.

One evening, he told me "Say yes." He then said something, and I replied
"Yes," not sure of what I'd agreed to. Everyone around us cheered. He'd
asked if I loved him, and would I marry him? Of course, that'd been
established previously. At a later time, he told me to put my hand behind
my back. When I obeyed, he put a ring on my finger. We were engaged!

He'd had difficulty obtaining the ring. Guy Calba took him to a jewelry store downtown. In a sort of black market way, he exchanged one
of his own rings, paid a lot, and, of course, threw in cigarettes to close
the deal. The ring looked so small, but was so large in reality. Love, that's
what it represented.

I didn't think of Gordon as coming from a foreign country—to me he was just "him." It seemed as if we'd always known each other. Practically every difference nameable separated us—age, nationality, religion, language, tastes, and ideas—yet we were so comfortable together.

I began feeling fearful over the detachment's pending departure from Nancy. The war picked up momentum and more troops arrived, swarming over the city in large numbers. The sidewalks now were full of sleeping or sitting soldiers—haggard and exhausted. Artillery fired constantly, but the Germans were withdrawing and all of Nancy finally was liberated. Château-Salins and nearby villages to the east also were free. Every day, I feared Gordon was going to move on.

We made our plans for the future—all in the sake of love. Mainly for now, we'd try to stay alive for each other. The Germans might come back—unlikely, but possible. Or bombing! I'd be careful. For Gordon, however, danger was constant. How afraid I was for him.

The liaison detachment had been stationed in Nancy two months when the day of their reassignment came. This was their longest stay in one place since arriving in France. After they left, I remained in the vacant house for awhile—crying, feeling empty, and so lost. I returned home to cry some more.

I returned to work, awaiting news. Father remained constantly in my mind. For months there'd been no word. We didn't know if he still lived. Now Gordon's fate was included in my fears. How I prayed. God must've tired of listening to all these women begging Him. But He wasn't quite ready yet to end it. The Americans who'd dashed across France in the summer of 1944 now were crawling toward the German border. General Patton, furious, had been stymied by long supply lines and insufficient gasoline for the Third Army, and by stiffening enemy resistance as the Germans reorganized after their debacle and retreat from Normandy. This now was changing.

The squadron had assembled at Château-Salins, located out in the country just east of Nancy. Nevertheless, this was an impossible distance as far as I was concerned. With no mail service or other means, we couldn't communicate. Two or three weeks later, Gordon came to visit for a few hours. They were moving again, but he didn't know where to or when. Everything was so illusive.

There was a sisterhood of waiting young women. We all kept in touch daily, in case anyone had news. Yvonne felt anxious for Charlie Leipersock, Lucette for Arthur, Raymonde for Joe, and Renée for her sergeant. Renée suspected he was married, but believed in his return to her. Even our friend Madeleine, knowing that her special friend (another sergeant) was married, kept hoping for his visits. I despised his attitude—having an affair while he had a wife back home in America—but I gave him credit for honesty, though one time I'd made an angry scene with him at his desk, spilling an inkwell. The other sergeant, however, left everyone in the dark. Most of the men came to visit, but Gordon, being the commanding officer, couldn't get away as much as the others.

One evening, I felt elation when seeing a jeep with their unit's insignia parked in front of Raymonde's house. I ran in. Yes, Joe was there, drying his shirt in front of the stove. Arthur had come with him. Did they have a letter for me? No. My heart sank, but there was an explanation. These two had left without Gordon's knowledge. While Gordon slumbered in his room, they'd tiptoed out and drove to Nancy in the open jeep, wearing no coats. They were soaked from the rain—their coats were in Gordon's room. Joe caught a bad cold from the excursion. But I was reassured; all was well. We had some other visits of this kind. Sometimes Gordon sent letters in this manner.

One Sunday afternoon, Arthur delivered a letter in the most interesting way by flying over our street. I ran to the balcony, as did

Arthur Pass and Lucette Fouillouse in the Americans' house near the landing field.

most everyone in our neighborhood. He yelled, "Hello, Nicky," from the plane's window, made another pass, and threw a message sack out. I dashed to retrieve it. He was good at this; the small bag to which a little belt was tied had landed right in front of my house. It contained letters for several of us—a most touching moment. As he flew over a last time, people applauded and shouted greetings to him. I was so happy with my treasured letter. It was full of love and dreams for our hoped-for future.

Arthur had dropped the letters in the same way that their reconnaissance planes delivered messages and maps to the troops. Sometimes, they dropped packets to isolated combat groups, or to units without radios or whose communications had failed. The small planes—Stinson L-5s—didn't have the prestigious appearance of the large bombers or the fast fighters, but their accomplishments were many. The pilots conducted observation and liaison missions with immense valor. When flying at altitude and seeing approaching German planes, the pilots dove their unarmed L-5s down to tree top level and hedge hopped to safety, avoiding enemy fire from the ground.

Nancy stood along a key route into Germany, thus American hospitals and rest areas were established here for the region. One of the main streets was reserved strictly for ambulances. It broke our hearts seeing medical vehicles pass by day and night, without break.

Thousands of soldiers had no place to go but the sidewalks, to sit and sleep. Snow and rain added to everyone's misery. Soldiers coming back from the front lines were covered in mud, from head to toe. They often only found a spot of sidewalk to sleep on. Local residents helped the best they could. Cafés, restaurants, stores, churches, and every other available space overflowed with tired and sometimes sick men. All over town, soldiers built fires in the streets, garages, everywhere.

The winter of 1944 proved most dismal. The ecstasy of the liberation and delight with the Americans began waning for several reasons. Food remained almost as scarce as during the occupation. The Americans were generous, but barely had enough for themselves because of the staggering number of troops and the difficulties in transporting supplies over long distances.

French people were freezing, with little or no coal available. We'd managed to restrain ourselves from cutting down trees, or burning good, sometimes antique, furniture. But to our disappointment, the Americans burnt anything they could find. We were saddened, but understood their great need.

Our deep love affair definitely lessened with the coming of the U.S. Seventh Army, which had landed as a joint American–Free French force in southern France several months earlier. The U.S. Third Army had been a group of angels in comparison. We weren't prepared for this onslaught. Excessive drinking was blamed for most of the problems. A number of the American soldiers seemed to think women were free for the taking. Actually, prostitutes were safer, as MPs were posted for their protection. Store owners and sales people were frightened for their property, even their personal safety, when drunken or wild-acting soldiers came in. Some men destroyed property when angered, most of the time due to a lack of communication, or haggling over prices, or the shortage of items.

I witnessed a violent outburst in a barbershop while on my way to the post office on Place Saint Jean. When just passing by, I heard gun shots, then the big front window crashed onto the sidewalk. People began screaming and running. The French police arrived, but several GIs held them and the barber at gunpoint. We never knew the reason for this disturbance. It didn't end until MPs took the men away, who grinned, laughed, and gestured when in the jeeps.

Numerous such incidents, including fights among the GIs themselves, became commonplace. Women walked in groups for safety. French people hesitated to visit cafés or restaurants for fear of an outburst. Once, two GIs gave Lucette and I long chase while we were on our way home from work. We were very frightened. Gordon gave me a bracelet with General Patton's headquarters address inscribed underneath, which I could show if getting into any difficulty.

Incredibly, we began missing the German soldiers' discipline. The unruly paratroopers in this army didn't endear us to our liberators. We felt unprotected. Their officers didn't appear to have any authority over them; actually they often joined them in their wild merriment.

French citizens, naturally, had invited GIs into their homes for dinner, especially on Sundays, but a father or husband needed to be present for proper decorum, of course. The exhausted soldiers were extremely grateful. However, when Mrs. Guissiani invited an African American officer, he said he couldn't come. When Cousin Gilberte asked another Black soldier, he pointed at the skin of his face. Black soldiers had been ordered not to interact socially with the local population. This prejudice was difficult for us to understand.

For all these reasons, in November and into December we almost felt as much distress as during the occupation. Then in late December, a rumor we didn't dare to fully contemplate began circulating—the Germans were holding on, and might return. The word Bastogne now was heard. On the map, the new German assault to the north in Belgium looked terribly close to us. Sometimes, the sound of artillery seemed to be coming closer. The American troops looked worn and depressed. Fear strangled us again.

Our city, full to the brim with American soldiers, might be a primary objective for the Nazis. Our fears, hunger, worries for loved ones, and disappointment in the behavior of some of the Americans removed the glow of our new-found freedom. We took pleasure, however, in not hearing German boots in the street and guttural voices around us. We'd regained our land, no matter how trampled. But what next?

For me, a ray of sunshine came with a surprise visit from Gordon—overnight only, but how marvelous. All else was forgotten. He was the loving, tender, quiet, gentlemanly person I lived for—so unlike those unruly soldiers I'd begun to dislike. From the beginning of our relationship, I felt he and I, despite our foreignness to each other, were like an island, isolated from all else. If we could only survive this storm and build our nest.

I practically lived only for his letters and visits, harder and harder to come by. Our parting was very sad. He had no idea when he could return, or where he was going. We knew it would be closer to Germany, the worst prospect of all. Mother and I were miserable—a legion of two in fearful wait.

Gordon's surprise visit was marred in one aspect, which later seemed rather humorous. I had a tooth pulled the day before. My mouth hurt terribly and my cheek swelled. I thought I looked so ugly. Our kisses were limited, as it hurt! Well, if we were to marry, he might as well see me at my worst.

He brought a most marvelous present—potatoes and coal. We cried with joy, and built a real fire and baked the potatoes on top of the stove. Heaven must be made of such treats. I expended several weeks of coupons for French bread, so he could take a full bag back with him—he liked it so much.

Gordon's visit caused a dilemma. With no man in our family living with us, he simply couldn't spend the night in our apartment. Our reputation would be ruined. Therefore, Gordon and I went to Lucette's house, since her father was at home, as well as her cousin, a priest—a definitely respectable arrangement. I slept with Lucette, but did tiptoe over to Gordon's room for a goodnight kiss. Lucette's cousin must've heard us; he gave me an affectionate wink in the morning.

By this time, I held a different job. In November, Lucette's boss had offered me employment at the *perception* (tax) office. I debated over this, being very happy with my current work at Maison Jacob. My pay, however, would be doubled and I'd be a government employee with good benefits. Mother officially decided for me. Being 17 years old, it wasn't mine to make.

I took the new job, and hated it. After a month of avoiding passes from the *percepteur* (collector), I asked for a transfer, which I got, but not for the better. Though the *percepteur* at the Perception de Vandeuvre didn't make advances, he despised Americans. His daughter had an American friend and he was miserable about it. Mr. Thévenet made my life miserable, too, after finding out about my engagement to an American officer. But I did my work well and he had no authority to fire me, especially since everyone in the office supported me and I passed my exams with high standing. Again, I unassumably delivered checks and cash to the central treasury. We called my boss "Molotov," as he had a striking resemblance to the Russian diplomat, and probably was just as hardnosed, too. This wasn't meant as an insult to Molotov at the time, because we loved and respected the Russians greatly.

Much of my learning about the adult world had occurred during these months. Joy and pain followed together at an accelerated pace in this period of my life. Every moment seemed filled with expectancy or fear.

The Americans established a public information office in an empty store, located about a half block from the Perception de Vandeuvre. Mr. Thévenet flashed black looks if any of us left too frequently for the lavatory. Thus, we took turns in going to the lavatory, at which time we also viewed the huge map in the news office window down the street. Flag pins showed the war front and indicated troop movements, all constantly updated by communication personnel. I avidly followed the Third Army flags, counting the kilometers separating the American positions from my father's location—near Dortmund, as mother and I still believed.

We faithfully viewed the map throughout the day. Ramie, an office mate, was engaged to a French officer held in a prison camp. She constantly checked the flag pins, as did Yvonne in the office next to ours. Her friend was a colonel in the Seventh Army. For most of us, this map provided the only means of obtaining current information about troop movements. Newspapers remained hard to get and didn't always provide such information, or presented it much later. Most of the time, the radio only played American "hillbilly" music, which most French people loved. It got on my nerves, however, and I came to dislike it.

When the sidewalk at the American information office became too crowded, people overflowed into the street, causing traffic problems as Rue Saint-Jean was a main artery. With so many of us having loved ones in military service or held in prison camps, we became friends when meeting here every day—all sharing hopes.

Sometimes, hostility was expressed toward women who fraternized with Americans. We were looked down upon by these people, especially by French males. They lumped us all into a group of girls with low morals, supposedly selling favors for chocolate and cigarettes. We weren't viewed much better than the women who'd fraternized with the Germans. Actually, a number of them were the same girls. I often resented the fact that some Americans didn't seem to mind this—that these women had consorted with the Germans. They couldn't say they didn't know, because many of these females still had shaved heads, obvious for several months. This was an insult to patriotic French people.

To avoid controversy, I stopped mentioning that my fiancé was an American. I only said my man was at the front. That way, people took it for granted he was a French soldier. It hurt. I wanted to tell everyone about him and our marvelous love—shout it from the rooftops.

Romances with Americans often weren't taken seriously, with good reason. Many soldiers promised marriage, but never returned. Also, there were cultural misunderstandings. To a proper French girl, a kiss sealed an engagement. French women learned, to the detriment of suffering many broken hearts, that Americans didn't view kissing as a binding contract leading to engagement and marriage.

In fairness to the GIs, all guilt shouldn't repose on their shoulders. They came to Europe fearful of the future and, after several months of savage combat, many were starved for affection. They faced the prospect of further hardship and possible injury or death, and were thrown into a culture that baffled them. Mobbed with hugs and kisses when liberating a town, a few weeks later they were expected to marry a French girl if they'd only kissed and hardly held hands. I'm sure we were puzzling. We flirted outrageously with them. How could we expect them to know our intentions and expectations? Of course, some Americans probably came to France expecting to find the "mademoiselles" of 1917–18 fame. Their fathers or uncles probably embroidered some magnificent tales about those World War I experiences. From my observations, most of the young men who wanted companionship found it.

My mother and relatives weren't really expecting my relationship with Gordon to continue after he left Nancy. In fact, I'm sure they hoped it would end. A broken woman mends—they were ready to cheer me up. But our relationship went on; our feelings for each other didn't lessen. We kept making plans to marry as soon as it was feasible. Our two concerns—the end of the war, and my father's return.

When my relatives realized this, they planned their campaign and went to work on me. They used every argument possible, but to no avail. The father of one of my friends even asked me into his office. He felt it his duty to talk to me as a father, since mine was absent, etc. I smiled, saying if this was all he had to say, I wasn't interested in listening.

Later, after Gordon started the marriage arrangements, an army chaplain met with me, giving a strong lecture about the problems awaiting us. Gordon and I already had gone over all this in great length—age and religious differences, my leaving France and family, his uncertainty about employment after the war, and many other things. Of some things we were certain. We needed each other, we wanted children, and we couldn't get much poorer than we'd been. I certainly wouldn't become hungrier. If we were to have problems, we'd work them out. None could dent our resolution. Grandmother was my powerful ally. Without her support, I might've not been so strong when facing everyone.

Our primary immediate goal was survival. I constantly feared that Gordon might be killed, injured, or captured. Daily life remained about as difficult as during the occupation. We were as hungry as ever, and mother suffered fainting spells from weakness.

Meanwhile, Gordon and I somehow contracted scabies! We never knew who got it first—we jokingly blamed each other. Regardless, we itched—to tears. A miserable experience! These parasitic mites are contagious, and easily passed on. I wore gloves at all times to prevent contaminating other people. We had to wash with the most awful smelling soap.

One evening shortly before Christmas, Arthur and Lucette came visiting. Arthur carried a letter for me, but from his expression, something didn't seem right. I read the letter. Gordon was letting me know he'd volunteered for a mission to Bastogne in a few days. If he didn't return, I was to have his belongings and get in touch with his family. Of course, he also wrote that he loved me. He'd contact me as soon as possible—if he came back.

The Bastogne battle—a sword poised over our heads! The Germans seemed stronger than ever, having built up their strength for a last great offensive. There's a tremendous difference in levels of fear—between a general apprehension in daily living, and the horror when heightened danger occurs. I definitely felt the latter. Arthur, having known the letter's content, felt saddened in handing it to me.

I spent the next days in pure pain—no Christmas pleasures for me. When would I know? How would I receive word? Our means of communication were so difficult. I simply sat numbed, and waited.

A few evenings later, I visited Lucette. Arthur was coming. I might get some news—whatever, I had to know. I sat with Lucette's father at the dining room table, trying to remain calm in anticipation of Arthur's visit. Lucette and her mother prepared dinner in the kitchen.

Silver Star

The month of December brought with it a determined enemy counter-offensive. In the process of counteracting the assault, very substantial U.S. forces were bottled up by the Germans in Bastogne, Belgium, including the 101st Airborne Division, elements of the 9th and 10th Armored Divisions, and the 705th Tank Destroyer Battalion.

Among the casualties were personnel suffering abdominal wounds. No doctor on the medical staff in Bastogne could care for this type of serious wound. Therefore it became necessary to somehow get a specialized surgeon into the pocket, for without immediate treatment certain death would result in many, if not all, of these cases. Volunteers were requested and Lt. Ancel G. Taflinger, one of the squadron's flying officers, courageously accepted the hazardous mission.

On Christmas Day, Lt. Taflinger lifted his slow, lumbering L-1 type aircraft into the cold afternoon air carrying the volunteer surgeon, Major Howard P. Serrell, who previously had never flown in an airplane. To assure the success of this flight, four P-47 fighters, returning from a mission, were ordered to escort Lt. Taflinger. During the 35 minute flight, he adroitly evaded heavy antiaircraft fire encountered over enemy-held territory. The P-47s continually circled the L-1 until the plane safely landed at dusk in a small field inside the encircled pocket. A 101st Division jeep awaiting their arrival immediately drove out to the plane and hustled the surgeon off to his urgent duties.

The P-47s, short of fuel, were forced to leave for their home field, making it necessary for Lt. Taflinger to return unescorted. He again braved heavy fire from the Germans on the ground and landed safely in his shot up plane after darkness.—Public Relations Office, *Month by Month with the Fourteenth Liaison Squadron, March 2, 1942 through V-E Day, May 1945* (Munich, Germany: Oldenbourgh, ca. 1945).

The doorbell rang. I tried not to move. Without getting up, Mr. Fouillouse said, "It's the newspaper woman. It's too early to be Arthur."

Lucette went to answer the door, then called me to come.

There stood Gordon—by the doorway at the end of the hall. I erupted! We ran to each other. I jumped up so fast I hit him, or rather hit my head against his helmet—hard! A bump stood on my forehead for a while. There are no words for such moments.

We then dashed to see mother. All was pure happiness. He was alive and I could touch him. That's all I wanted. He could only stay overnight, but time had no meaning. The waiting had been long; all that was erased.

He'd flown a surgeon and medical supplies across enemy lines to the encircled troops in Bastogne. For that, he'd be awarded the Silver Star by General Patton. I was immensely proud of him.

In January, the Germans finally met defeat in Belgium when American reinforcements arrived and the weather cleared, allowing planes to support the army. From then on, the flags moved fast on the map, and finally onto German soil. Gordon couldn't visit much, but he could now send letters through the mail. They'd been reassigned to Luxembourg, and soon Germany. We wrote a lot, and kept on planning.

He felt anxiety about being sent to the Pacific for the planned assault on the Japanese mainland. I mostly dismissed this, being too weary of worrying. It remained in a corner of my mind, but my main fears were for the present.

One of the planes was missing—Charlie Leipersock hadn't returned from a mission on December 24! He must've been shot down. This hit close to home. Yvonne Roth, who considered herself his fiancé, fell into despair. She'd also contracted tuberculosis. Theirs was another example of disrupted lives in wartime. (After the war, Charlie never reconnected with Yvonne. She eventually recovered from TB and became engaged to another man.)

I also became greatly concerned about Lucette. Arthur stopped visiting her, but this might be understandable—none of the men could visit us when assigned to the advancing front toward Luxembourg and the German border. But he didn't write to her!

December 24, 1944

T/Sgt. Charles W. Leipersock took off in his L-5 type aircraft during the afternoon from a field in Luxembourg on an operational mission carrying Major Rudolph M. Jordan of the 10th Armored Division. Neither returned from the mission and they are considered missing in action, presumed to be the result of enemy action.—*Daily report.*

May 4, 1945

S/Sgt. John Usinger returned from a flight to Landshut, Germany, and reported that T/Sgt. Charles Leipersock, a liberated POW and former member of this squadron, was there. M/Sgt. Joseph Maheux went in his plane to bring him back to our field. When they returned, Leipersock was greeted by everyone; we were all glad to see him!

He related his story in part: "We had been well briefed before takeoff and understood the dangers of our flight. While in the vicinity of Ettelbrook, Luxembourg, we were shot down by flak and the plane was afire. I told my passenger to jump. My face was covered with blood and I couldn't tell if he did jump or not. I have never seen him since. A Mark III tank crew captured me immediately upon my parachuting to the ground. I was taken to Bitburg, and in a couple of days to Nurnburg, thence to the Stalag Camp at Moosburg, Germany. I refused to do any work. I had to walk from Nurnburg to Moosburg. The hardest experiences I suffered were from hunger. En route we traded for things to eat with German farmers and Russian, French, and other forced labor displaced persons. Started receiving Red Cross packages while at Nurnburg. Used some of the candy and cigarettes to trade with. Weighed 190 pounds when captured and after four months dropped to 150 pounds. Was liberated from the Moosburg Prison Camp by III Corps troops of the U.S. Third Army on April 29th. General Patton was there to speak to the men who were formerly with him in Africa and Italy."

Leipersock took a bath, the second in 4 months, was given a change of clothing and a hot meal. Spent the night with his buddies and the next morning returned to the field where thousands of Allied POWs were being evacuated.—Public Relations Office, *Month by Month with the Fourteenth Liaison Squadron, March 2, 1942 through V-E Day, May 1945* (Munich, Germany: Oldenbourgh, ca. 1945).

She begged me to ask Gordon about it. I found out. I had to be brusque to her—Arthur had decided to end the relationship! He couldn't marry her, with him being Orthodox Jewish and she Catholic. This caused both of them much pain for many years.

Lucette turned suicidal—for a few days we watched her night and day. Her parents said, "I told you so. You're just one of thousands." But my mother, with her gentle ways, helped a lot. After a painful time, Lucette pulled through, but said she couldn't see me anymore. She wanted me to understand this—I was too painful of a reminder of what'd happened. I hated losing her friendship, but I understood. Afterward, I'd watch her from a distance. She eventually began going out again, meeting a nice American soldier. (They soon married and eventually lived in Denver, Colorado.)

In May 1945, we met at Place Stanislas. Lucette told me of her engagement and asked about Gordon, but we didn't speak for long, both claiming we were in a hurry. She did say she still loved Arthur. It was most distressing. I would've liked to move mountains for them.

I tried it years later, but again fate stood against them. In 1955, Gordon visited Arthur in Boston and found him unmarried, and regretting having left Lucette. In 1956, Gordon and I visited Lucette in Denver. Her husband had died. We called Arthur, but he'd just got engaged—after all those years.

War Brides

With Europe so impoverished by the war and so different from anything the GIs knew, they naturally turned to boasting about America. Such boasting is expected—actually a "must." Love of home is natural. But some soldiers exaggerated, giving a wrong impression as to the reality of their personal lives. Gordon hadn't been guilty of this. He'd painted a rather somber picture of what I should expect.

According to what many GIs said, however, it seemed as if everyone in America had big cars, large houses, lots of money, fancy clothes, all the conveniences one could dream of, and more. Europeans appeared so dingy, poor, and downtrodden to them. Lucky girls marrying them would find themselves in paradise. Many future brides became ecstatic.

On the other hand, I was a little disgruntled. Gordon said he didn't own a car. Strange! Why not?

He said his family lived simply. How come? He appeared well educated and was an officer! I became puzzled.

When I corresponded with his mother, in one of her letters she mentioned making cornbread and seemed pleased about it. This alarmed me. In France, no one but possibly the poorest of the poor made their own bread. In fact, I'd never heard of anyone who did. And Gordon's mother in Scottsburg, Indiana, said "cornbread." But corn wasn't eaten by people—only by chickens and pigs. Strange indeed! Not yet 18 years of age, I was sure only love counted. When other girls enumerated what they expected, I just kept quiet and hoped for the best. I'd get Gordon and be poor. Well, for a time we were.

Europeans, too, were rather misled by American movies, showing the United States as a land of riches with incredible opportunities and where women lived like queens. As a result, it took little effort for GIs to talk some young ladies into marrying them—especially after so many years of deprivation.

La Sardine de Marseille—"The Sardine of Marseille" that becomes a huge fish! People from Marseille are known throughout France for exaggerating. All countries have such localities famed for boasting. In the United States, Texans are known for it.

Jimmy Vaught, a soldier from Amarillo, Texas, became engaged to my friend Huguette Zint. A good, normal Texan, Jimmy was vocal about the Lone Star state's huge farms, and highways without end, full of cars. All very true, but none of this bounty belonged to him personally. Like most Americans used to open spaces, and never lacking food or clothing as we did at the time, he began telling my friend Huguette about bountiful Texas. Also like most soldiers, he expected to go home, find a good job, and fulfill his expectations. He didn't lie; he simply dreamed aloud.

Jimmy and Huguette got married. He returned to Texas after the war; she was to join him later. But he couldn't find work. How to tell her that she couldn't join him? There wasn't room for her in a shack occupied by his parents, the brothers and their wives, and children. He wrote to her honestly. I translated the letter, since Huguette couldn't read English. It was so difficult, but she loved Jimmy. Pregnant, but full of courage, she went anyway. They succeeded in Amarillo, eventually raising five children and having grandchildren, and achieving middle class prosperity.

It worked out for Jimmy and Huguette, but I believe that many GIs reneged on their promise of marriage for many of the same reasons that Jimmy honestly stated. These soldiers broke engagements not because of their lack of care or love for their fiancés, but because they'd cornered themselves into their own dreams.

1945

The big guns no longer were heard, and Nancy wasn't as crowded with troops. The Allied armies had moved into Germany. Free French soldiers were seen everywhere—what joy! The collaborators were punished—but not punished enough, and not enough of them punished, we felt. Glory to our heroes of the *Résistance*! To our surprise, we learned that some people thought to be collaborators actually were *Résistance* members or had aided them. We now felt embarrassment, having doubted their loyalty.

Afterward, I learned that our long-time friend, René Lunot, was one of these people. As police chief, he seemingly collaborated with the Germans; in fact, he openly encouraged this conception, even to his wife. Becoming disgusted, she divorced him. His mother also disowned him. Following the war, it was revealed that René actually was a top leader in Nancy's *Résistance*. In fact, most of the Nancy police were anti-German, though appearing to collaborate with them during the occupation.

Newspapers began circulating, and a little more food became available since the Germans weren't looting it anymore. Pierre Laval, the senile Marshal Pétain, and their Vichy clique were removed as pride slowly replaced our shame. Best of all, we knew the Nazis wouldn't return.

Soon, large numbers of French prisoners would be liberated from German camps. A few already were coming back, but this proved rather disquieting. Their experiences aged them so terribly and their attitude wasn't what we expected, but of that I will speak later. The sight

René Lunot leading the police band after the war.

of the few returnees caused anxiety to those waiting for husbands, fathers, sons, and brothers. Mother became terribly concerned, but I, as young people do, thought "Not my father"—he wouldn't be like them. I believed he'd be exactly the same person who'd left us in 1939. Nevertheless, I felt concern about his reaction to my marriage plans.

Engrossed in my own little world, I didn't pay much attention to French politics at the time. Much debate occurred as political factions formed—socialists, parliamentarians, Gaullists, nationalists, even communists, who'd played such a prominent role in the *Résistance*. As all deprived people do, everyone wanted everything in the new Fourth Republic (established 1946). All I wished for was Gordon and father. I suppose this was mostly what the average person wanted—their loved ones safe, and also good French bread, croissants, and chocolate.

Spring came, with the flags on the map moving ever more often. People screamed with joy when the Allies liberated areas where relatives were known to be held. We had no real idea about when or how each would return—direct communication was non-existent. Some released prisoners found rides in American, British, or French vehicles, or were flown out. Some simply seized cars, motorcycles, or bicycles, coming back on their own. Some even walked, but mainly they returned by train.

When people knew their relative was in an area recently taken by the Allies, they began waiting for them at the Nancy railroad station—sometimes for days. As trains full of returning men arrived, people in the crowd endlessly asked about fathers, brothers, sons, husbands, friends. Waiting family members held up placards inscribed with their relative's name. Joyful shouts burst out when families were reunited, and distressing screams when told someone wouldn't be coming back, or, if eventually returning, might be in a state practically worse than death itself.

With father being held in northern Germany, we had to wait longer. Finally the flag pin moved to Dortmund. Nearly a year had passed since we'd heard from him, but we hoped. I cannot describe our feelings. Wild with excitement, we cleaned house, went to the beauty shop, found food for a feast, and told relatives the news. Waiting proved practically unbearable. As a guess, we thought he'd return from Dortmund in about two days. We took turns—with one of us standing among the crowd at the Gare Saint-Jean, while the other stayed home in case he arrived by other means than train. But a week went by without father returning. We worried even more.

Then one morning, after getting our hair done again, mother and I went to the station. Around noon came announcement of the arrival of a train from Frankfurt. An incredible mob waited. Mother and I stood almost in front, close to the gates.

Men began stepping off the train—the dirty, dazed, tired, mutilated, and sick remnants of the strong, vital, healthy men who'd said goodbye more than five years before. We stood rooted to our spot—horrified, stunned, silent. Then the shouts of joy and pain began. Then we saw father. My whole being exploded in relief! Though looking 60 years old instead of 42, he was whole. He'd seen us. He smiled, with tears running down his cheeks. It was him, as I knew in my hopes he'd be. He'd shaved, and walked upright and proud; not a skeleton like some, but full-bodied.

His strong arms squeezed us until we held no breath. We couldn't speak. We just grasped each other and began walking out of the station.

We took the tram home as there was no other means of transportation. He was extremely tired, but excitement held him up.

Our indescribable joy lasted but a short time. Then pain began—his, and then ours through him. The first frightening thing occurred when we asked him how it felt to be standing on the soil of France.

He replied, "It betrayed me; it will pay!" We were shocked!

He also said, "There's nothing left of me. If you don't want me, I'll go away."

After waiting these many years…we didn't know how to reply! After all our efforts to beautify ourselves, he also said he didn't like our fancy theatrical get-up. To our horror, he mixed German words, which we despised, with his French.

When arriving home, he sort of collapsed. We wanted to serve him lunch, but he couldn't eat, saying his stomach was so damaged (he had ulcers). We then realized his extraordinary physical effort in coming to us when getting off the train. Mother and I looked at each other in despair. We just hugged him in silence, then the three of us sobbed for a long time. We cried over our years of separation and pain.

Then he said he had some things to take out of his bags. This showed us we hadn't lost all of him. The knapsack was the same he'd left with; his razor the one we'd sent him. He'd used it that morning on the train. There was a ski cap I'd made for him, and his copper pot (which I still have). He gave us gifts (I can't recall exactly what; I'm sure I've blotted these items from memory because I hated them so much— they were German objects). He had German bread with him and said he liked it. He couldn't know how much this hurt us—we who'd scrambled to get fresh French bread every day in case of his return, thinking it'd be the first thing he'd ask for. We stood numbed—the wall of pain ever building.

Mother remained speechless, but I exploded. I told him we couldn't bear any thing German, even a single German word! He looked astounded, crushed. He then said that I, even mother, surely had German boyfriends. That did it. I fully went into rage. Mother kept silent, deeply hurt. We realized the awful truth that Nazi propaganda had done its job even better than we'd thought. The people they didn't burn in the ovens they brainwashed.

But our love was strong. Mother and I swore to each other that we'd work on this. We had much catching up to do—more than five years. We'd get my father back no matter what. We'd exorcise the Germans from him. We resisted them before and could again.

They'd made the prisoners believe that the French people were pro-German and happy, living a good life under them. Mother and I would tell him the real story, but good! They'd convinced the prisoners to believe the Americans, British, and Free French were invaders, unwelcomed by the French population. We'd have something to say about that, at least I knew I would!

I began fearing father's thoughts regarding Americans. He said he'd walked all the way from Dortmund to Frankfurt. Didn't any Americans offer a ride, I asked? He said he refused; he wouldn't ride with them. I was horrified—I, who couldn't wait to tell him about my marvelous love. Mother whispered to me, wait awhile.

But father's tenderness remained despite the garbage heap of Nazi propaganda he'd lived under. When looking at each other, love was still there, as well as the fact we'd all managed to survive. Yet, the happiness of the victory over the Germans was gone; it seemed they'd won in our house. I heard their boots again; will until my last day. I couldn't forgive and cannot forget.

I fully grew up that day. That afternoon mother and I sat helpless, watching father sleeping on the couch. We were so terribly happy to see him, but terrified about our life to come. How were we to cope with his pain and ours? We whispered, since he seemed to be sleeping so soundly. We decided that we must, in all fairness, tell him about Gordon. We also needed to explain what our life had been like during his absence, and we must know what his was. The fog must be cleared or we couldn't survive as a family. We whispered about a big party planned with the family. We didn't know right now what to do about that—we'd wait. A good idea came to us—grandmother could fix our problems! She always did, didn't she? She'd help us communicate.

Father woke up; actually, he acted like he did. We should've suspected he wasn't asleep, but only pretending. I suppose similar scenes occurred simultaneously all across France after prisoners returned. He honestly admitted listening to everything we'd said. He felt relieved and tremendously happy at our joy upon his return, and the fact that we loved him so much we didn't even leave the room just so we could look at him. He'd been so afraid we wouldn't want him. The Nazis had convinced the POWs that they weren't wanted in France, but viewed only as cowards for losing in 1940. We now understood why he'd said he go if we didn't want him. What had been done to him?

We all hugged again; maybe there'd be joy after all. But blow after blow followed. He stood up, calmly picked up Gordon's photo on the desk, and handed it to me, telling me to throw it away. He said the subject wouldn't be mentioned again—that was that! But it wouldn't be for me; I'd go to war! I'd win this fight. Though too young to join the *Résistance*, I'd heard plenty indicating that people could struggle and win when having enough reason and ambition to hang on. I had plenty of both.

Next, father told us not to hope grandmother would have any influence on him about anything, she being a woman. He wouldn't listen to a woman—another Nazi victory, as they considered females entirely subservient. Regarding my uncles, he didn't want to see them, since they'd had a good life being at home, etc., etc. He didn't want to tell us about his years in Germany, and didn't wish to hear about our lives. What was past was past, and that was that!

Yes, mother and I had a problem on our hands. We prepared a macaroni and salad dinner. He asked where the meat was. We said we hadn't been able to get any. At first, he expressed anger, then surprise. Our first stab at resolution was made. He didn't know we'd missed meat, or butter, or so many other things. He'd wondered why we were so thin. He had much to learn. When he did, it was too much all at once.

Our friends, the Guissianis and Kronemakers, came up to celebrate, carrying wine and a very small cake that Marguerite managed to save for the occasion. Mother and I were relieved by the feeling of normalcy they brought with them. Much love was exchanged, but, of course, I worried about father's reactions. Our neighbors wanted to know all that had happened to him, but he said little. They bombarded him with their news—Mr. Guissiani's jailing by the Germans and the beatings, Pierrot joining the back-country *Maquis* fighters, Mr. Kronemaker's exploits as a railroad saboteur, etc. In a few hours, father learned much about how he'd been misled, but there was a long way to go.

The next morning—another trial! As mother and I prepared to go to work, father got up and asked what we were doing. We told him. He said "No," we were women and wouldn't be working anymore. He was home now, and it was his duty to support us. Besides, why should we work? We were supported by the government, weren't we? Another shock—we needed to work! What we received from the government only fed us one day of the month if that. Alright, we could go today, but he'd see his former boss where he'd worked before the war. He'd get his position back and then we'd stay home as good women should. Women staying at home, yes, we'd heard that from the Germans, and Vichy, too. With heavy hearts, mother and I stepped out the door.

When arriving at the office, more dismay. My friend Ramie was in a state of shock regarding her fiancé, a French officer held by the Germans. He'd returned, but with a German wife and child. Another score for the Germans! Waves of hate swept over us.

When mother and I returned home, we found father in despair. Yes, his former employer welcomed him with tears of joy. Yes, he could have his job back…when sugar, chocolate, and such were again available, which hopefully would be soon. The boss's son had died during a *Résistance* operation. He told my father about former co-workers who'd been killed by the Germans.

Then father went to look for a new suit. He was told he needed coupons, but it was the high price that astounded him. He also stopped at a restaurant where he could only get some salad without oil. He was learning about what life had been like, and still was, for us. We now knew we needed to be patient, providing the most happiness we could rather than being angry at him. He simply hadn't known these things. He'd wondered why we hadn't mailed him the items he'd asked for when a prisoner, but now he knew why. He began feeling guilty. I think this was worse.

But he wouldn't give in. Grandmother came, and he didn't want to see her. Never put off by anyone, grandmother talked to him anyway. She told him what needed to be said, which we couldn't do. He sent her away, but he'd heard.

We began telling him about the Jews and also his friends who disappeared. He rejected this as American propaganda, or Gaullist, or communist. He wouldn't believe it. We ourselves didn't know all that much about the full horrors of the Holocaust, but we did now that people we knew were brutally taken away for little reason or pretext, then tortured or even shot. We didn't know how many had disappeared, or the state they'd be in if they returned—the few who did.

Father joined a club of returned prisoners. Pleased, we thought it would do him some good. We were wrong. They supported each other in believing we lied to them, covering something up—they weren't sure what. France conspired against them, but they did volunteer to help out the less fortunate returnees who were ill or handicapped.

One day in May, train loads of concentration camp survivors arrived in Nancy for repatriation. Father's group went to help—they saw, and then they believed! I met these returnees up close, too. They were brought to our treasury office to be registered, and given identification cards and money. They still wore the coarse, striped, prisoners' clothes later so infamously remembered from photographs and films seen by people in Allied countries.

It absolutely broke our hearts. We were shocked by how ghastly they smelled from the conditions they'd lived under. Some were alert, responsive, and so glad to be free, but others couldn't eat or swallow, and could hardly talk or reply to questions. Some were amnesia like—they couldn't remember their names, where their homes had been, or who their relatives were. For identification purposes, we assigned them new names. We sobbed when turning our backs to do the office work. Some couldn't hold their new identification cards and money in their hands, so we pinned the little packet holding these items to their shirts. These were the ones in relatively better condition; they could walk, somewhat.

They needed washing, doctors, and feeding in a city with barracks and accommodations already overflowing with Allied soldiers. American servicemen were magnificent in helping them with ambulance and jeep rides, and in any way possible. For several days we lived with the full recognition of the hell some people lived and died in. This was beyond our worst expectations—we thought we knew it all, but we didn't.

Our Jewish neighbor, Mrs. Pinnel, also returned, but with a grossly enlarged bulk, apparently due to cruel German medical experiments. She could only mumble, and died a few months later. Mr. Frank, the furrier, also came back after the war. He showed me his back, horribly lacerated and beaten. He, too, died several months later. The Grundfelts and Mr. Marick, the other Jewish furriers mother also worked for, never returned.

How I needed Gordon at this time. I hadn't seen him for two months or received a letter since a few days after father's return. The war had continued in its last stages in Germany. I was so afraid, but couldn't talk about it with father at home. I did manage to speak to mother—I began to panic.

Then one day, I accidently noticed a letter in father's coat pocket. I exploded! Yes, he confessed he'd collected my letters at the mailbox. He gave them to me. Yes, that man must care for me considering the number of letters he sent, father said with his dry humor. But he must stop sending them as he was wasting his time.

Afterward, mother watched the mail and brought letters to me at work. Father wasn't budging on the subject. I was desperate. If Gordon came to visit, father said he'd throw him out. What was I to do? Even grandmother couldn't make father budge on this matter. I was helpless, lonely, heart broken. Until the age of 21, I couldn't marry without my father's consent.

I also was concerned about mother. I didn't know exactly what my parents' personal relationship was, but I could detect tension and sadness between them. I could also sense father's desperation. Physically he was improving and getting stronger, but mentally he was deteriorating. Anger raged in him—anger at the discoveries he was making about the German occupation and what had happened. Violence erupted in him. We became afraid to bring up subjects that brought on flare-ups.

These could be caused by small things, such as when he asked: Why did we break some tiles in the kitchen? We didn't; we told him they cracked during the hard winter of 1940 when we couldn't keep the house warm enough. He hit the tiles so hard he broke some more.

At times he'd cry like a child, and then one day it finally came—he began telling us what the Germans had done to him. He told us of his years as a POW, which he had tried so hard to forget when stepping off the train, hoping they'd disappear.

Father was on the Maginot Line when the great German offensive finally came. He was trapped, along with thousands of French troops. They resisted the best they could with small arms. To their horror, the big guns couldn't be turned around and were absolutely useless as the Germans came from the south, behind the Maginot Line.

After their capture, the POWs were marched into Germany. For seemingly endless days they walked toward the east without food or water; they were beaten and some shot for the smallest infractions. When passing through towns and villages, they were spit on by German civilians. Rocks, bottles, and other objects were thrown at them. They suffered atrociously; their feet in such pain they could barely move. Near Dortmund, they were held in large pastures with no shelter or facilities of any kind—so crowded they could hardly move. The stench suffocated them. Some died of thirst and hunger. Father was a strong man, but with a tendency for strep throat and bronchitis afflictions. For days he was delirious with fever.

Dysentery hit the camp, a further horror for the prisoners. As more prisoners arrived, the Germans began to remove the ones able to walk, putting them to work in factories. These men were considered fortunate. It was slave labor, but they'd have a semblance of shelter and a little food. Father managed to look fit and able, becoming one of the so-called fortunate. For several weeks he managed to hold his tongue—a miracle, really, for such a strong willed man. The incentive to keep quiet remained strong, however, as terrible punishment was meted out to the insubordinate.

But spontaneous errors can sometimes arise almost unconsciously. The men began singing as they worked. The problem was the song itself, the *Marseillaise*. The Germans' anger knew no bounds. They herded the singing group out, and, as an example to the other prisoners, beat them senseless. Some died or were so crippled they were shot. The survivors, father among them, were sent to a special punishment camp, with conditions so bad they wished they hadn't survived the beatings. This camp included prisoners of many nationalities—English, Polish, Belgian, etc. A strong bond grew among them—a brotherhood of the helpless. They couldn't escape, though it constantly was on their mind. The camp was too well guarded.

They worked in a quarry—atrocious, grueling labor. Winter was coming, one of the worst ever recalled in Europe. Father's heels froze, which would cause him pain for the rest of his life. For shoes, they wrapped rags around their feet.

As horrible as this experience was, it may have saved father's life. Had he remained in the factory, he might've been killed in the Allied bombing that destroyed it later, or succumbed in typhus epidemics that killed many prisoners.

When their three months of punishment ended, the men were sent to various other work places. Father was among the fortunate ones assigned to farms in the area. This also might've saved his life. He'd have sufficient food and somewhat decent treatment, plus shelter and some warmth. Father's group included an Englishman, and several Frenchmen and Poles. They decided that to survive they needed to learn German. This would allow them to communicate with each other and the German people with whom they'd be in contact. Father learned German quickly and well, making him the intermediary between the Germans and the prisoners. In a way, this designated him as the leader of the group, plus the fact that he'd tended a small farm in his youth and had knowledge about livestock and gardening.

The farm wasn't large, and their small group could manage easily. The farmer was in the German military, leaving a household of women comprised of his wife, mother, and children. These were tough, hardworking women, not the gentle, city-type females such as my mother whom father had become accustomed to. His mother, indeed, had tended their small farm in Savigny, but she was a small, dainty, pious woman.

For years, father lived and worked on this farm outside of Dortmund, speaking mostly German, becoming accustomed to this kind of agricultural life, and somewhat admiring the tough rural German women. These Germans viewed the French as weak, playful, cowardly, and pretty much a useless people, unworthy of contempt. Their consideration of the British, too, fell along similar lines. Later, American airmen were viewed as hired murderers, Chicago gangsters, and such. As the Allied bombing took a toll, it wasn't hard for the prisoners, seeing so many of their own killed in the factories and cities, to also consider the Americans and British as enemies. As father related this tale, we now understood much of his attitude.

Nazi propaganda had convinced the German people, and many of the prisoners, too, that the *Wehrmacht* occupied European countries as friends, allowing populations in conquered nations to set up decent, good governments of their choice in the "New Europe" (Pétain, to the prisoners, was still an upright, valorous hero of the past). Nazis claimed they'd attacked in "self-defense" against hostile nations surrounding them. German propaganda also claimed that civilians in occupied countries lacked for nothing and lived a quiet, pleasant existence under German protection. If the prisoners had qualms about things remembered from the beginning of their capture, they were told it'd been done for their own good, since even their own countrymen viewed them as cowards and no longer wanted them. The POWs, isolated from outside news, somewhat believed this. Those who managed to escape and avoided being killed naturally wouldn't be coming back to inform the other POWs about real conditions. Letters from home also didn't reveal anything since all correspondence was heavily censored.

Father was surprised and sad when we didn't send him things he requested—chocolate, soap, etc. He had no idea we couldn't get these things for him. He soon thought we didn't care about him anymore. Thus his reaction when first seeing us at the train station.

Our independence as working women proved to be a particular dilemma for him. Even though German women worked hard physically, they were absolutely dependent on direction from men and looked up to them. Now, father had to depend on us for a living. Though he returned to his former employer, the pay was so little he continued to rely on us. With France having experienced enormous changes in social attitudes and the workplace during the war years, he didn't feel at home. He resented finding himself adjusting and revising his views.

Now, we better understood aspects of his behavior, but we still loved him. But this didn't make daily life easier. True, at the beginning of the war, he despised the Nazis and was willing to fight them with all his might. He'd warned us to protect ourselves against them. But his original views of Germany and France were eroded by four years of masterly Nazi propaganda.

He possessed a gun; we feared what he might do. (Some time later when father got to know Gordon, I came home from work one day and found them discussing their side arms, which lay on a table. They were only comparing firearms as military men are prone to do, but I was shocked. I talked to Gordon on the balcony, saying I worried about father shooting collaborators.) In fact, a rash of crimes occurred in Nancy during this period, in addition to the summary actions against collaborators. Violence might flare up when a returning POW or forced laborer found a wife had taken up with another man during the occupation, or there was a property dispute, and so on—crimes largely due to disrupted lives in wartime.

Father returned to normal in some aspects—he did the cooking, especially since we worked. He'd close the kitchen door when preparing meals. We weren't to go in. He also planted tobacco in the garden.

Little by little, understanding on both sides grew, but too much damage had been done. For mother, the deprivation, hard work, fear, and misery of the war, topped by the disappointing, painful return of my father, took its toll. She grew close to having a breakdown, but needed to continue working. She could take just so much. If father kept venting anger at himself and the new life he had to face, she couldn't endure it. Their relationship crumbled. I watched helplessly. I had my own pain and battle to fight.

Father was willing to accept Germany's guilt, as well as France's faltering steps in the war. He was beginning to assent to change, but wasn't yet ready to accept de Gaulle and the Americans or their political views. For the communists, the attitudes of the returning POWs were a pot of gold furthering their cause and they tapped it to the utmost. At the time, the monumental political struggle continued in forming a new national government to physically and morally rebuild France. Granted, the communists were very prominent in the *Résistance*: What would their role be in this reconstitution? They couldn't be left out. They needed to receive their due, but how much? Unexpectedly, many former POWs fell into their lap. Their anger proved a boon to the communists—a powerful tool in the national debate.

Father began attending meetings with other former prisoners. When the communists soon took over these gatherings, father returned home angrier than ever. Mother and I now needed to keep him from attending to prevent his outbursts of pain and sorrow. Neither mother nor I cared or knew much about the political storm raging at the time. But we knew one thing: Father was suffering greatly from anger stirred up by the communists' political views.

We enlisted the help of father's long-time friend, Mr. Gauche. We arranged for Mr. Guache to "accidentally" drop by and see father on evenings when the meetings were scheduled. Or, we'd arrange to go somewhere with father and keep him from getting back in time. We lived on a tight rope.

Mother's health wasn't good—she'd had fainting spells and heart problems before. She now began faking a few swoons at appropriate moments. Though greatly ashamed, she used the tools at hand. Actually, she didn't fake too much because our difficulties often triggered her illness, whether she wanted it to or not.

I needed Gordon so much. I received his letters—father no longer hid them from me. In fact, one day father brought one to the office. I was deeply touched, seeing father's gesture of love and affection. Father, however, tested my strong feelings for Gordon by bringing home a young man who'd been a prisoner himself. He was pleasant and handsome, but of course I wasn't interested. That plan failed.

One happy day, Gordon wrote that very soon, with the war ending, he'd return for us to get married. I read the letter to my parents. Father responded by ordering me to immediately write to Gordon, telling him not to come, or if he did, father would simply throw him out. I told Gordon about everything occurring at my home; we agreed we'd find a way.

The war ended on May 8. How we rejoiced. Not quite as much as during Nancy's liberation, but we were extremely happy. Gordon now would be safe! I just had to wait for him to return—and then we'd face father.

I set up a plan in a letter to Gordon. When he arrived in Nancy, I wanted him first to call me at work and request that I leave because mother was ill. Then we'd go to my home together and meet father. An illness in the family was the only valid reason allowed by my boss for us to leave work. That week, our office was extremely busy exchanging occupation money for French currency—a big job.

About mid-afternoon one day, a phone operator informed me that father had just called and wanted me to come home immediately because mother was ill. I became terribly frightened—I felt I'd been caught at my own game, but this was real if father had called. I ran so fast I could hardly breathe, wondering how ill mother might be.

About halfway home: Who should I see coming toward me? Gordon! I was astounded. How'd this happen? My father had called! We kissed, holding on to each other in the street. We were so happy. After all these months, I needed him so much.

What had happened? Simple. Gordon disregarded my request to call, went directly to my house, and met father, who didn't throw him out after all. Gordon said father wasn't unfriendly and tried to speak in German, thinking Gordon might understand it from interacting with Germans, but he didn't. They even poured a drink together. Is there such a thing as miracles!

Father seemed to have perceived our scheme and went to make the call himself. (We didn't have a telephone at home—we made our calls at the corner Café Chez Roth.) Imagine mother's surprise when coming home and finding Gordon and I. All our weeks of anxiety over this were gone! We were truly happy.

Gordon only had a few days off, thinking we could marry right away as in the United States. But this couldn't be; not in France. *Bans* needed to be published for 11 days. Gordon was disappointed, but the next day we went to the city hall to publish the *bans* and make preparations for the wedding, scheduled for June 16. My happiness knew no bounds. What words could be used? I didn't have them.

Gordon returned to Germany with plans to come back on June 15. I worked a few more days and submitted my resignation. Then I busily made wedding preparations. It was to be a simple affair, yet much needed to be done. For one thing, we needed to find food for the feast! That was a major operation. What was I to wear, and mother, too?— another major undertaking.

During my frantic activities, I thankfully hugged father whenever passing by him. I knew that meeting Gordon face to face would change father's mind, but I didn't expect it so quickly. Gordon wasn't one of those noisy, undisciplined American GIs that were so wearisome.

I realized how my parents felt about their only child going to America. I'd be leaving France, and was sad, too—it's always been a sorrowful part of my life. But it was a choice to make and I made it. Above all, my dear parents wished for my happiness, regardless of their pain in seeing me go. They exhibited great love and affection toward me—it was most bittersweet for them.

June 15–16, 1945

The sun is shining and my world glimmers with joy, love, and marvel of all kind. Everyone and everything around me is good and beautiful, adorning my happiness. I suspect tomorrow will be even happier—it will be my wedding day! But I'm so happy today. I don't see how I can get even happier. How can the flowers be any prettier, the sun brighter, life nicer—I'm walking on air!

Gordon arrives. I touch him, look at him—can't stop. He feels so good, so right, so everything. Tomorrow I'll bear his last name—a strange name I can barely pronounce. That's a small matter—just so long as I can have it.

He has a surprise for me. When I embrace him, he asks me to touch his shoulder. There are two bars instead of one; he'd been promoted to captain. What a nice wedding present. We have so much to celebrate—our whole being is a celebration. We can hardly believe that the moment has arrived after nine months of handicaps, obstacles, and fears, but here we are, smiling like sprites in paradise.

There is so much to organize—our household is full of food preparation, hustle, and bustle. Gordon and I stand on the fringe, holding hands on the balcony, and waiting for even more magic. Is time standing still, or moving too fast, or too slow? How can time be measured when someone is so full of every precious moment and can't wait for more? I count the minutes toward the next day, but also can't bear for the present moments to disappear.

A long, beautiful evening arrives. We stand on the balcony along with father, who is determined to keep us company. In his mind, privacy for us will begin tomorrow. Today we can hold hands. (I believe now that father wanted to keep me just a little longer.)

A little later, mother contrives to give us a few moments alone to say goodnight and dream of tomorrow. Good night—tomorrow we begin our long years of everything together.

Saturday, June 16, we wake up—if we slept. With so much to do, we hardly have time to bathe in our joy. Our small apartment fills with people, preparations, and excitement. There is so much joy in our hearts, but first things first. I go to the beauty shop. Gordon leaves for downtown for some last minute errands—mainly to find transportation.

Our tribulations aren't over. My hair is in rollers and I'm under the dryer when the electrical power goes down low (vestiges of wartime remain). My hair won't dry! Time is flying by—we must arrive at the Laxou city hall by 3 o'clock for the civil ceremony. At noon, with damp hair, I come home.

Everyone is frantic—no flowers! Did Gordon know of the French custom that the groom provides the flowers? One of my friends, Yvonne Roth, dashes to the florist just to be sure. If Gordon got some, we'd have two sets—we'd be safe. Our apartment overflows with people setting the long table for our wedding feast later in the day. The kitchen and every other room remains busy—we have to dress, etc. Actually, I'm in the way. I become quite anxious about Gordon getting back in time.

He arrives shortly, without flowers or transportation! Horrors— Yvonne got the flowers, but what about transportation? How are we to get across town to Laxou for the civil ceremony, then to downtown Nancy for the religious service? We talk to Mr. André, who operates a taxi service. He can't help us, saying only doctors, ill persons, etc. can ride in a taxi. We'd have to walk!

I set my hair and try to eat a little (I can't remember if I could swallow). We get dressed. The moment is near. Now, off to city hall. We set out, walking through the field where I'd played and picked flowers when a young girl. We pass by the house where we lived when I was 2 years old. We all arrive at city hall, even Aunt Suzanne with her two canes.

The mayor, wearing a tricolor *sache* and beaming with a joyous smile, is very courteous and even provides a translator, who repeats everything in English. This is a nice gesture, not to be forgotten. We agree to everything the mayor tells us to be, and to do. We sign the certificate—now husband and wife—almost. We now proceed to the American Chapel at 5 o'clock for God to marry us.

Transportation? Our party boards the tram—to the surprise and delight of the other passengers. We walk through crowded Saint Jean street to the movie house, Nancéac, which has been requisitioned and turned into a chapel. It is soberly but beautifully decorated.

No translator here. I'd somewhat memorized my parts in English and repeat the best I can, when signaled. I must've done alright because we were definitely married. For real, forever—by God and the state.

The sidewalk throngs with well-wishing friends and many curious bystanders, blocking the street. The big crowd gives us an ovation. Ours is the first American-French wedding remembered in Nancy since World War I. Another American-French couple marries right after us. Later, these marriages become so numerous that no one takes notice. But we create excitement on this day.

Gordon has managed to acquire a car for some of us to ride in, but most take the tram back to our house. There, we feast for hours. To everyone's amusement, Gordon prefers beans, which mother has cooked for him. With all of the prepared delicacies, he favors beans. We drink and sing, and, of course, grandmother sings. My little Cousin Gilbert sings *Lily Marlene*. All is a joyous fog for me. My only clear thoughts are about making our escape to be alone.

It's French tradition for the bride and groom to be detained as long as possible, with people creating ploys to prevent them from leaving. But it's also understood that a "traitor" among the guests will make arrangements to help them escape. We'd set this up with Madeleine Kronemaker, who'd put her new baby to bed. She sends me to go and check on him. Instead, I dash for the recess of the garages and parking lot, half a block away. Shortly, Gordon leaves, checking to see what's taking me so long. Of course, we don't return! What great fun this is.

"Our portrait, taken two days after the wedding."

Finally alone, we happily walk arm in arm toward the city center, to the Hotel Thiers, the best in Nancy. The evening is beautiful—sort of twilight. The nicest thing occurs as we reached Avenue Foch. The street-lights come on! Nothing unusual? Yes, it is—very much so! For the first time in four and a half years, Nancy's streetlights are turned on again. This is a wonderful omen for us. It's just for us; there's nobody else on the street. We reach the hotel with all the happiness possible for anyone to possess.

Postscript

Not many months later, mother realized her differences with father were irreconcilable. She filed for divorce and moved out of the Blvd. Foch apartment. Theirs was another example of lives broken by the disruption of war. Mother never remarried, but father eventually met and married a Polish woman—a concentration camp survivor.

Odette Mangeot, who daringly assisted Mr. Bérin and the *Résistance* in rescuing the downed airman, patiently hoped for her husband's return from Germany. Shortly after her husband had been captured early in the war, she realized she was pregnant. Unfortunately, the child died at a young age. Her husband didn't know of the pregnancy or the child's death. She hoped her husband survived in German captivity as a POW. His return proved a joyful reunion, despite the sad news Odette had to relate. They soon had another child.

Pierrot Guissiani, my *FFI* hero, eventually married, thanks to my fortuitous involvement. One day I asked Pierrot to attend the theater with

Guissiani family members after the war—(l. to r.) Pierre, Gerard, Marguerite, and Micheline.

me. As young men are prone to do, he said he wasn't interested. But I prevailed, and he went. As chance would have it, backstage I introduced him to my friend Nadine, the ballet dancer at the conservatory. Not long afterward, they married, and eventually raised a large family in Algeria.

Gordon remained assigned in Europe for two more years, during which time I mostly resided with mother at her new residence (in Essey) between his visits. I discovered I no longer was a French citizen! According to French law, I'd lost my French citizenship by marrying someone of a different nationality—supposedly, I was solely a U.S. citizen, though I'd never set foot in America. I found it impossible to get permanent work since jobs went to French citizens.

For a month during this period, I traveled to the squadron's head-quarters in Germany and secretly hid out in Gordon's room—a spec-tacularly luxurious setting. The squadron officers occupied a grand mansion of the Krupp family, Germany's great industrialists and former manufacturer of armaments. The estate included expansive lawns and gardens.

Only Gordon and a very pleasant German maid, who spoke French and quickly became a good confidential friend, knew I was there. However, I eventually was found out in similar fashion as when meet-ing Gordon in the Americans' kitchen in Villers. When solitarily walking outside on the Krupp lawns, I looked inside to the banquet room and spied bread on a table. Seeing no one around, I stepped inside to snatch some. But I wasn't alone. Off to one side sat the squadron's command-ing officer. I was found out! But all turned out well.

In September 1947, it was time for Gordon and me to go to America. Along with 13 other passengers, we boarded a merchant ship in Bremerhaven, Germany. The ship's hold contained still-serviceable tanks being returned to America. One of the passengers was a concentration camp survivor—a solitary woman, deeply affected by her harrowing experiences and who kept to herself.

After we arrived in America, Gordon remained in the air force for a few more years and we resided at military bases in the midwest and southeast. When Gordon resigned from active duty, we moved

"Pregnant with my first child, I stand next to the flag mast when leaving Bremerhaven for America."

to Chicago where he attended the University of Chicago. In 1952, he started a long teaching career in business administration at Washington State University, as well as serving in the U.S. Army Reserve.

Pullman, Washington, remained our permanent home, where we raised a daughter and four sons. I continued my education, then taught art and French in the public schools. In time, mother and French friends came to visit. I also opened an art gallery, displaying some of my own paintings and those of other artists.

I returned to France seven times—visiting mother, father, and relatives, seeing dear friends, and revisiting those places where sorrow and joy changed us forever in our *Season of Suffering*.

September 9, 1994
Commemorative newspaper article in the *L'Est Républicain*, Nancy.

The First American Lands in Field...

Former bomber pilot, transferred to artillery observation, Captain Taflinger lands at Villers-lès-Nancy in his Stinson.

Photos of Captain Taflinger bring back memories of Villers Liberation...

Because of his interest in flying since his early youth, Jean Dehant witnessed Capt. Taflinger's landing on September 18, 1944, a few days after the liberation. Jean Dehant...saw the plane circling over Villers. "It was obvious he was searching for a suitable landing field. When I saw him descending I took my Kodak 6/9 and dashed to the landing site"...

"Apparently Taflinger landed here, because the Essey airfield was being bombed at the time." Responsible for a liaison squadron, Taflinger and his Stinson set down at Placieux"..."Strangely, in June 1940, a German observation plane, a Fiesler Storch, made the same maneuver as Taflinger, but I didn't have a camera with me to record it," said Dehant, feeling much emotion recalling his American friend.

Captain Taflinger...married a Laxovienne, Nicole Braux... Before they left, Jean Dehant exchanged addresses and has saved all the correspondence, very precious to him. "We spent many evenings together, with Taflinger and his men who lived in an empty house in Villers..."

Making use of Jean Dehant photos, the *Committee d'enfants patriotique of Villers* [former POWs, Algerian veterans, etc.] will retrace the liberation of Villers.

The festivities will take place Sept. 15–18, 1994.